2-25-94

THE CULT
OF REVOLUTION
IN THE CHURCH

The Cult of
REVOLUTION
in the
CHURCH

John Eppstein

ARLINGTON HOUSE·PUBLISHERS
NEW ROCHELLE, N. Y.

Library of Congress Catalog Card Number 73-18470

Manufactured in the United States of America

Library of Congress Cataloging in Publication Data

Eppstein, John, 1895–
    The cult of revolution in the Church.

    Includes bibliographical references.
    1.   Revolution (Theology)   2.   Violence—
Moral and religious aspects.   3.   Social ethics.
I.   Title.
BT738.3.E66   261.1   73–18470
ISBN 0–87000–241–4

1793051

CONTENTS

Part One

CHARACTERISTIC FEATURES OF THE CULT

Chapter 1
THE CHALLENGE

For the first time in the history of Christian civilisation, revolution is presented today as an essential, if not *the* essential aspect of the social mission of Christianity. Marxist priests, propelled as they imagine by the wind of history and seeking to reconcile remnants of their religion with a social dogma which knows no God, are not alone in this pretension. There are other theologians, Protestant and Catholic, busily engaged in justifying the thesis that violence is a necessary means of social progress and reform. The purpose of this book is to examine the causes and manifestations of this extraordinary aberration, to subject the so-called "theology of revolution" to a critical analysis, and to restate the pacific and rational alternative to this notion of continuous social conflict which the true Christian social order offers.

There is, alas, nothing new in Christians fighting and killing one another and other people in a political cause or even a religious cause. The Crusades against Islam lasted intermittently for nearly a thousand years. Before they ended, the Reformation had resulted in the bitter wars of religion accompanied by the mutual persecutions of Protestants and Catholics, the aftermath of which (as in Northern Ireland) is still with us and does not lack exploitation by professional revolutionaries. This feud, in turn, combined with national rivalries, overflowed into the colonial wars of the 16th and 17th centuries. In the 18th century first the American Revolution (in origin a British civil war), then the more radical French Revolution introduced the vogue of insurrections and wars fought for general political rather than religious theories. Soon, however, these were identified with the principle of nationality, giving rise to a whole series of armed rebellions for national independence in the Americas and in Europe. Meanwhile the idea of a world revolution to overthrow the existing social order, sown in France in 1789, germinated and culminated in the Communist Revolution, first in Russia, then in China, the dynamic influence of which is now felt—and resisted—in every continent. While Communist exploitation of local nationalisms has characterised most of the many actual or phony "wars of liberation" and subversion during the period of decolonisation, the outcome of the bloody Civil War in Spain was a striking instance of successful national opposition to the progress of the World Revolution.

Now, throughout this grim story, equally compounded of self-sacrifice and heroism, and of egotism, ambition for power and cruelty, the honest man, and in particular the Christian, has had a choice to make. His choice—between taking part in or resisting armed rebellion or revolutionary war, just as the statesman's decision for or against resorting to war—and the same applied to the Papacy when it claimed temporal jurisdiction—may have been objectively right or wrong. But the decision, private or public, was judged by a standard, often imperfectly understood or hypocritically interpreted, but always appealed to—as indeed it is to this day, not least by unbelievers. And that standard is natural justice.

Was it right or wrong to fight for the Parliament or the King in the English Civil War? Was it just or unjust for the North American Colonists in 1775 to join in the revolt against the British Crown, or, as the United Empire Loyalists who trekked into Canada after their defeat, to defend the British connection? What did conscience require of the Frenchman, priest or layman, when confronted with support of or resistance to the French Revolution, as it evolved from its moderate constitutional beginnings into the climax of the Terror? Which side to take in the European revolutions of 1848, and on which side of the barricades to be in the Paris of 1871? Or in the Mexican Revolution of 1905, or in the Russian revolutionary wars of 1917–20, or in the last fratricidal Civil War in Spain? And so on, to the present day with the agonising choice of the Vietnamese villager, the African tribesman in the borderlands of Portuguese Guinea, the Southern Sudanese or the citizen of Northern Ireland. In all these cases and many others individuals, and particularly fathers of families, have had to take a position either for or against rebellion. The bloody American Civil War of 1861 was no exception. Obviously fear and calculation of probable failure or success influence the decision, but there is also always the question of duty and of what men believe to be the justice or injustice of the opposing causes—or, maybe, the injustice of both. That is how human nature is made, original sin and all. Men cannot be wholly unconscious of the moral law.

Now it has always been the function of the Church to guard and expound this law, engraved by God in human nature and reinforced by revelation. It has, in relation to society, certain inescapable precepts concerning the mutual rights and duties of all members of the human family, such as the duty to keep faith, to contribute to the common good, to respect duly constituted authority—without which no political society can exist —and to safeguard the rights of individual persons and families, which is the proper purpose of that society. All these have their bearing upon the conditions which may in exceptional circumstances justify, as a last resort, war or violent insurrection. But what matters most for defining the ethics of revolution is the Divine command in the Decalogue, "Thou shalt not kill." For revolution, like international war, inevitably involves killing people and, as we shall see later, organised killing whether ordered by a government or by insurrectionary leaders has always been seen by the Church as the human act most difficult to reconcile with the law of God, even in a world riddled with original and actual sin, and therefore to be restricted to the case of absolute necessity. Whatever the circumstances, the rule "It is never lawful to kill innocent people"[1] is the unchanging bedrock of Christian tradition on this sub-

---

1. *"Numquam licet interficere innocentes."*

ject. We cannot have a better criterion for judgment in this whole discussion than that recently proposed by Cardinal John Wright:[2]

> I offer the thesis that in a period of social turbulence, indeed revolution, those who are committed to "openness" and needed change on the level of things human are doomed to be blown about by every wind of doctrine, unless they have a commitment not less certain to fixed principles of faith and morality. . . . The faith provides the absolutes concerning God, the person, the honor of God and the dignity of the person, the value of life and the primacy of the spiritual as Christians must see these always and everywhere.

It is part of the self-deception of the Christian advocates or excusers of revolution[3] to pretend—contrary, as we shall see, to the consistent teaching of the popes including John XXIII and Paul VI—that it does not necessarily involve violence. But there is no political revolution known to history—whether justified or not—which has not involved a measure of civil war and provoked forceful resistance; which means that people on both sides, and in between the contending factions, are wounded and killed. One can indeed read through the spate of books which have been poured forth lately on this subject without once finding such abstractions as "violence," "revolution," or "liberation" expressed in terms of the actual human beings who suffer from them—the homes destroyed; the families divided against one another; the men, women and children terrorised and killed; the soldiers and police who lose their lives; the "liquidation" of the defeated class or faction; the submerging of all distinction between combatant and non-combatant which the frenzy of civil war invariably brings and the dreadful legacy of hatred which it bequeaths. Yet every human being, from the poorest African or Asian peasant to the more fortunate citizen of an industrialised Western state, has

---

2. *The Church: Hope of the World*, Prow Books, 1972, p. 128.

3. E.g., Joseph Comblin in his important book *Théologie de la Révolution* (Editions Universités Paris, 1970) to which we shall refer in the following pages. See also the report to the World Council of Churches of the *Conference on World Cooperation for Development*, 1968. Section 1 (17).

an immortal soul—each, as Jacques Maritain said, "a spiritual universe"—created by God and potentially redeemed by Christ; and therefore enjoys personal rights which are sacred, the right to live most of all.

There may indeed be just rebellions in the future as there have been in the past. But it takes a powerful amount of good to be attained, as well as reasonable prospects of success, to justify initiating a campaign of organised violence in view of the price which human beings have to pay. Self-defence is a natural right, which Our Lord's precept of non-resistance to evil, as a counsel of perfection for the individual, does not overthrow. Consequently to join in defending one's country against external attack or internal subversion; or to defend oneself and one's fellow citizens against intolerable oppression by those who wield authority; or to aid those who are thus defending themselves, are the only sure causes which can make it lawful, and may make it a real social duty to resort to the minimum of armed force necessary for the purpose, unless some other remedy is available.

That is the consistent conclusion of the Christian tradition and of natural reason which the Second Vatican Council confirmed, saying:

> When public authority oversteps its competence and oppresses the people, these people should nevertheless obey to the extent that the objective common good demands. Still it is lawful for them to defend their own rights and those of their fellow citizens against any abuse of that authority, provided that in so doing they observe the limits imposed by natural law and the gospel.[4]

But this judgment, and all that we have said above about the difficult choice which men have had to make and may have to make again between supporting or opposing an insurrection, can only be understood as referring to *particular situations in particular states in view of the actual circumstances of time and place.* This is true of scholastic teaching on the subject

---

4. *Gaudium et Spes*, 74.

beginning with St. Thomas' famous text upon tyranny[5] and of papal teaching on the subject, of which Pius XI's encyclical of 1937 on resistance to the Mexican persecution is the most explicit. Whatever the objective merits of judgments about particular cases, peace being the first social objective of the Church, as it is the first and most essential requirement of the family—which is the foundation of all human society—these cases have always been treated by the moralist, until now, as the exceptions, the tranquility of order being the right and normal social condition.

The challenge with which we are now confronted for the first time is something entirely different. One can only describe it as an almost institutionalised, permanent, continuous process described as The World Revolution, with which the Church is called upon to identify herself, as against the elements of society variously described as the bourgeoisie, imperialism, reaction, neo-colonialism, capitalism or even American domination.

"The revolution of which we are to treat," the Abbé Comblin begins his massive treatise on *Théologie de la Révolution,* "is the world revolution which rises above the horizon of this latter part of the 20th Century and which nothing is likely to prevent exploding in the 21st Century. It is the revolution of the proletarian nations."

Despite this rhetorical beginning (which prompts one to ask who are these proletarian nations and against whom they are to revolt), this author proceeds to a full and often perceptive analysis of the many forms which revolution has taken in the past and is now taking in order to plead his curious thesis, which is: that the history of the West is the history of progressive revolutions. From this he leads to a well-argued but fantastic theory, which we shall examine in Chapter 5, that political revolution is the real message of the Prophets and of the New Testament. Jesus Christ, despite all his recorded sayings to the contrary, despite his refusal to lead a national rising against the Romans and restore the kingdom to Israel, despite indeed

5. See page 150.

14

the whole tradition of charity, forgiveness of enemies, forbearance and loving kindness, which the very name of Jesus evokes for many millions and which has given Christian civilisation its distinctive ideal, was really a revolutionary.

> Undoubtedly, [this author writes] Jesus did not himself wish to use violence, nor did he want his disciples to have recourse to it. . . . The revolutionaries who do not exclude violence cannot claim to imitate Jesus, but they do appeal to the dynamism of his message and the context to which it belongs which is the Old Testament.

Thus, as we shall see, scriptural contrasts between the rich and the poor, the mighty and the humble are made in this thesis not to enjoin spiritual dispositions ("Blessed are the poor in spirit"), or duties of social charity ("Sell all that thou hast and give to the poor"), or the virtue of humility ("Behold the handmaid of the Lord"), but to serve the class war of Marxist theory and the assumed confrontation between the rich and the "underdeveloped" peoples of the world today. Certainly the hollowness of worldly power and glory has been a constant Christian theme, despite the Church's deference, sometimes excessive, to temporal authorities. Certainly there are mutual obligations of justice and charity for all members of the human family which are consequences of the Christian message, among them the duty of the wealthy to help their poorer brethren, to which so much importance is nowadays rightly given on a worldwide as well as on the local scale. But it is a different matter to empty the Christian religion of its supernatural and spiritual content and give it a unique political twist.

This caricature of Christianity identified with the contemporary slogans of the Left and propagated by ingenious theologians, Catholic and Protestant, is swallowed by many young Christians, or ex-Christians, uncertain of their ground, who are only too ready to find in it some moral justification for accepting revolutionary propaganda, be it of Soviet, Maoist, Trotskyite or Marcusian vintage, to which they are constantly subjected; justification, too, for resorting to violence on behalf of any cause, academic, industrial, racial or political, which the militant agitator may choose for them. Whatever the merits of theories recently evolved concerning genetic origins of innate aggressiveness in man and behavioral differences, we are forced to conclude from all known history that there is in all men, tainted by original sin, a tendency to violence. Everyman is a potential Cain. It is an urge, individual or collective, to attain a desired end quickly, by any means, riding roughshod over the rights and interests of one's fellow men and the restrictions of law and custom. Pride, greed, envy, lust and ambition for power all are only too ready, in our fallen nature, to reinforce this instinct to smash the obstacles to the desired end; as indeed, on the other side, is generous indignation untempered by prudence. That, in the sphere of politics, is the spirit of revolution, all the more potent when the end is presented as good, such as liberty, fair shares for all, or the overthrow of oppressive authority. And it is invariably the invitation to destroy—with all the hatred involved in the process—rather than to construct, which makes the greater appeal to our innate violence. The great sin of the intellectuals who are now trying to prove the essentially revolutionary character of the Scriptures is therefore that they are removing the one great inhibition to this human instinct of violence which the spiritual force of Christianity and its ethical standards represent. That is the pastoral consequence of the "theology of revolution."

Chapter 2

THE CLIMATE OF VIOLENCE

"Violence has become a social, contagious disease; it unleashes acts of criminal folly; it organizes conspiracies of secret and cunning connivance; it takes up arms in a spirit of revenge, to embitter, not to settle quarrels among peoples. It spreads abroad the opinion, devoid of hope, that violence is an ineluctable necessity. It renders the whole of society doubtful of its inner solidarity; it discourages the effort to work boldly and harmoniously; and it disappoints the hopes of many for a truly better world. We must react spiritually against the temptation of such discouragement which could prove fatal for us and for the future generation. We should reaffirm resolutions and programmes of industry, of concord and of manly and civil peace. Let us strengthen in the people the sense and the taste of uprightness and goodness; let us uphold the initiatives and institutions working for the common good." —Pope Paul VI, May 20, 1973.

The whole problem with which this book is concerned, which is the choice between the tendency, on the one side, to excuse and justify recourse to violence for social ends and, on the other, the Christian imperative to "do violence to no man," must be viewed in relation to the climate of opinion and behaviour in our several countries, and especially in the advanced countries of the Western world, at the present time.

It would not be possible, for example, to ignore the traumatic experience, especially in the United States, of the long war in Vietnam. For all wars, whatever their justification, inevitably have a brutalising effect upon many who are caught up in them; the more so when, as in this conflict, systematic terrorism on the one side and the practical impossibility on the other of distinguishing between combatants and non-combatants, and the massive use of modern weapons, caused such a terrible toll of innocent lives. Moreover, television and the illustrated press, by giving incessant publicity to it, to an extent unknown in any previous war, inured millions in every country for years to a daily diet of violence and death. It must be remembered also, as part of the political history of this epoch, that there has never been a war, with the possible exception of the Spanish Civil War, which thanks to the emotions stimulated by the mass media, was so successfully exploited to advance the propaganda of the Communist cause throughout the world.

Yet, quite apart from the psychological effects of wars, it is an undeniable fact that, despite the welfare services and the high standard of living, despite also the vast development of national education systems, there has been in the last ten or twenty years, within our own countries, a staggering increase in the statistics of violent crime. The reports of the London and New York police, for instance, have the same sickening tale to tell—more assaults, more damage to property, more murders, more robbery with violence, and particularly more rapes year by year. The latter had increased by 50% in London in the first six months of 1972. A Gallup Poll in the United States, published in January 1973, showed that one person out of three in the centres of big cities did not feel safe at night from mugging or robbery. So far as statistics are available, the number of such personal crimes of violence is not so great in the Latin countries. There has indeed always been a good deal of the brutish and the cruel in the lives of the slums and ghettos of great cities, from Dickens' London onwards. But, though there are parts of our Western world, such as certain Negro quarters in the United States, where squalor and frustration account for a high proportion of personal crime, it is not the violence of the poor which is the most remarkable feature of these ugly police records today. All classes are well represented, the middle and upper strata of society, and particularly the young intelligentsia, accounting for the majority of violent acts which have

18

a political flavour, the terrorism, the hijacking and also the baneful prevalence of drug addiction.

This phenomenon, however, is not the most serious aspect of the matter. The majority of people do in fact lead normal lives free from violence and, though it is disturbing to recognise this increase in the size of the law-breaking and anti-social minority, it need not have fatal consequences for our society provided the majority is sustained by a sound morality based upon the natural law. But it is not. A generation ago one could say both of the positive law and of the generally accepted standard of personal conduct in countries of the European Christian tradition, that they were basically moral and rational. Peregrine Worsthorne, in a thoughtful article on "Why We Bow to Violence,"[6] writes of the attitude of earlier generations to violence:

> Not only did they know it as a real evil, but they lived in a culture which affirmed it as a theoretical evil. The life of reality and the life of imagination combined to rub home the lesson that violence was dangerous and ugly.

Mr. Worsthorne is inclined, I think, to exaggerate the extent of actual violence in the period between the two World Wars which he has chosen to compare with the present day, but he is right in pinpointing the radical change in the climate of popular opinion:

> How different it is today. A contemporary child is pampered and cosseted in the home from earliest infancy, where his parents slave around him; indulged in the school, where the teachers are forbidden to lay a hand on him and where bullying, once rampant, has been largely eliminated; pandered to in adolescence by a whole commercial structure designed to react enthusiastically to his slightest whim, so that he reaches maturity accustomed to getting his way. . . . But alongside this protracted training in indiscipline goes a cultural diet that promotes the belief that violence is the highest form of human expression, the quickest and most direct way of getting things done, irresistible to women, the only civilised response to a stinking society, the

6. *Sunday Telegraph*, London, August 13, 1972.

sharpest instrument of freedom. For every taste and inclination and every level of intelligence a good justification for violence can be supplied pretty well on every bookstall and in most evenings' television entertainment.

The systematic popularisation of violence, particularly on the mass media, is no doubt a proximate cause of the collective resort to force and brutality nowadays by groups of workers or students whose predecessors, no less passionately aroused a generation ago, would have held back from it. Mr. Worsthorne recalls one of the worst incidents of the former lately in England in the course of an unofficial strike of dockers:

> . . . those terrifying pictures on the television screen of docker pickets armed with bill hooks, first knocking down the police at Scunthorpe and then brutally kicking them in the head. How did this nightmare scene come to be enacted in the affluent society of 1972? The General Strike of 1926, when industrial strife was far more passionately intense than it is today, witnessed no comparable acts of such calculated brutality.

Violence on Television

The influence of television in fostering the acceptance of violence, and more particularly the selection and presentation of current affairs by newscasters, has been the subject of many studies. Educators concerned with the formation of children's political concepts and attitudes are particularly concerned with this subject since it is the almost universal conclusion of investigators (e.g. in American, British, Australian, French and German schools) that television has now become for most children, even before the secondary school level, the most trusted authority about national and international events—more important than teacher, family or church. Dr. Judith V. Torney of the University of Illinois, in the course of a paper on "The Influence of Current Affairs Broadcasting upon Pupil Attitudes towards Politics,"[7] writes:

7. Presented to the 9th Atlantic Study Conference on Education at Bordeaux, September 1972, on "The Interaction between Television and World Affairs Teaching in Schools."

The decision about what is sufficiently newsworthy to be shown communicates to the child. The major kind of international or foreign event that the American child sees on television news is war or violence (Vietnam and Northern Ireland) . . .

She quotes Mr. I. Charmy's description of the latent communication of the TV about violence and war:

The newscasters tell us in their baritone-rich voices how many of us have killed how many others of us and, betraying a covert kind of excitement, the announcers give us the subliminal message: "Well, folks, it's happened again and it's always going to happen, and there isn't a damn thing we can do about it."

This is indeed one of the most important factors in creating the prevalent climate of violence because of the ubiquitous presence of the TV in the homes in all the advanced countries. It means that whatever other influences impinge upon life, we are all at the mercy of an immensely powerful agency for which conflict, warfare, riots, crises and human tragedies always have priority over the less newsworthy portrayal of peaceful and normal life because of their sensational news value. It is not that there is evil intention on the part of newscasters or commentators. They are the victims of a system which grew out of sensational journalism. They work in a terrible hurry, which makes a fair selection of news difficult. Explained M. Christian Bernadac, editor of the Third Channel on French TV (ORTF), to the Bordeaux Conference: About a hundred films pour into his service every day, in addition to shots and stories from his own photographic teams; and twenty or thirty of them would be about the war in Vietnam. No wonder no balanced picture of the world emerges in the TV news.

No less powerful, and more culpable than the news coverage for the vulgarisation of violence, is the tendentious presentation of entertainment and discussion programmes by the progressive establishment which now predominates in broadcasting. More no doubt by instinct than design, everything which flouts tradition or defies authority, whether moral, political or educational (e.g. university students and professors), can count upon favourable treatment if not prominence. By the

21

same instinct the majority of foreign commentators in the sophisticated as well as the popular press in Anglo-Saxon countries, when writing about others, habitually work on the assumption that the Left is always right—be it in Brazil, Spain, Portugal, Turkey, France, Italy or the U.S.A. It is a kind of professional religion of revolt.

Such are some of the more obvious day-to-day influences which operate to fortify rather than counteract the habitual acceptance of violence and approval of revolution.

The Moral Law Abandoned

What is the deeper explanation of this intended or careless encouragement of the cult of violence in the many agencies which feed the public imagination and popular sentiment—television, radio, cinema, press, paperbacks and the theatre—not to speak of academics who play to the gallery? First and foremost is the assumption that Almighty God is either non-existent or irrelevant and that there is no objective standard of right and wrong. What criterion then can one apply? There is no human substitute for the fear of the Lord which is the beginning of wisdom. For a little while, maybe a decade or two, social convention or a sense of decency, formed by the habitual acceptance of Christian standards in the past, can act as a restraint upon the public pandering to sensuality and brutality. That was the case in England until about 1950 in regard to sex, for the monogamous Christian family was the traditional principle of the law of England in these matters. Then, on the plea of a spurious liberalism, diligently propagated by the small, well-organized British Humanist Association and its derivatives, there followed in rapid progression laws for easier divorce; the legitimation of homosexual practices; the partial permission, ending in the wholesale distribution, by the National Health Service of contraceptives; the weakening of almost every legal restraint on obscenity on the stage, in films and in books; the Abortion Act; and now the campaign for euthanasia. The very courageous attempt of the Catholic Lord Longford and his Commission in 1972 achieved only a minimal effect in their effort to stem the flood of pornography, for they took as their standard of permissibility the prevailing public sense of common decency. But how could this be determined and how sanctioned? The only real argument against fornication and all the apparatus of visual stimulation which surrounds it—as the Devil knows very well —is that it offends the law of God and the whole Christian tradition concerning the dignity of woman and of the human body as the temple of the Holy Ghost. Throw that away, as our secularized societies are doing without even the restrictions upon immodesty and lust which some of the Eastern religions and the tribal traditions of Africa impose, and there is no barrier to degradation left. How right was Pope Paul VI when he said:

> We must realize that we are living in times when human animality is degenerating into unrestrained corruption; we are walking in mud.[8]

But what has this rake's progress of sexual licence, which can be recorded *mutatis mutandis* in the United States, Sweden, Denmark and other post-Protestant countries as well as in Britain, to do with the problem of violence? It has a great deal to do with it, on two grounds. First sadism, a vile product of the enslavement of the mind and imagination to sex, soon produces themes, pictures and stories, particularly in the abundance of pornographic paperbacks with their lurid covers as well as in plays and films. Here is an additional invitation to personal violence of a particularly vicious kind because it involves inflicting cruelty for pleasure.

Flouting the Sanctity of Human Life: Abortion

The second and more serious contribution of the campaign for "sexual freedom" to the atmosphere of violence is in its establishment of abortion as a social institution. Within five years of the passage of the Abortion Act in the British Parliament which, despite a few nominal safeguards, virtually pro-

---

8. General audience, September 13, 1972.

vides abortion on demand, 160,000 girls and young women, the majority unmarried, were being aborted each year.[9] There are parts of the United States which have followed this example; and the astonishing decision of the Supreme Court to annihilate restrictions upon a woman's demand for abortion is in danger of making prenatal infanticide a national institution. In the Netherlands the introduction of legal abortion is being vigorously contested by Catholics with English help. Opposition to it in France continues strong; in Federal Germany the battle is joined; but it is undeniable that in many countries it is the abortion propaganda of the humanists which is making progress. There can hardly be a worse form of violence against the human person than the dragging of the unborn infant out of its mother's womb with forceps or by suction, to be thrown into the incinerator. It illustrates in an extreme form the contempt for the value of individual human life, created by God, in the supposed material interest of society; which contempt, in a different context, characterises the propaganda and behaviour of the revolutionary, whatever the ideology, class, nation or race for whose triumph he believes the individual to be expendable.

The Idolatry of Political Causes

Indeed, the complement to the denial of God himself, which we have seen to be basic to the whole climate of violence, is the denial of the personal worth of man. And it is here that many Christians, lured into the field of political action for revolution at home or "liberation" abroad, are among the worst offenders. An habitual blindness to the human rights of individual men, women and children characterises the idolatry of political causes. For instance the militants of a number of Catholic Justice and Peace Commissions, such as those from

---

9. In this matter at least, unlike the muted and divided witness of the Catholic community on contraception, the Catholic bishops, priests and people have been vocal and persistent in their opposition to the Act. The Society for the Protection of Unborn Children is a rallying point for Catholics and non-Catholics alike. In April 1972 the Society organised an anti-abortion rally of 80,000 people in Liverpool. Another rally of 100,000 followed in Manchester in March 1973.

Western Europe brought together at Brussels by the enthusiastic Marxist Canon Houtart in October 1972 to foment the guerrilla campaign against Portuguese Africa, never look at the evidence of human suffering inflicted by their proteges. Nor do their colleagues of the World Council of Churches, who have been no less zealous in their support of the North Vietnamese against the Americans. Stories, often untrue or exaggerated, of the malefactions of the other side and of the "repression" which subversion inevitably provokes, whether in Uruguay or Bolivia, Africa or Southeast Asia, serve as the emotional pabulum of these seemingly generous crusades, which warm the self-righteous hearts of distant radicals. There is no fair balance of evidence, still less an examination either into the necessity of the resort to force or its actual impact upon families or individuals. It is basically the same disregard of the rights of the person which has marked the more violent student rebellions—now happily on the decline—in European and American universities. "The cause" excuses everything:

> A call to destruction in openly anarchist style; contestation of every rule and every value in order to increase confusion; . . . continued renewal of violence apparently aiming at nothing but destruction; constant resort to mob excitement, so as to drown the voice of reason or charity; these were the methods applied during six weeks of unforgivable disorder in the full glare of publicity.

That is the comment of the Egyptian philosopher, Mirrit Boutros Galli,[10] on the Parisian student revolt of May and June 1968, which certain French Dominicans found so much to their taste and which *Témoignage Chrétien* and other Catholic progressive publications took as the occasion for preaching violent revolution as a Christian duty; as they continue to do.

Now it is true, and of great importance, that 90 per cent of the French university students wanted to complete their studies, and had and have no part in these excesses. There are many other centres of student unrest in other countries where

---

10. *Tradition for the Future*, Alden, 1972.

that is certainly true of the great majority also, just as the trade union pickets who resort to brutality in England are a tiny minority of the workers involved in strikes. But the importance of these developments is twofold. First, they exemplify the fact that revolutionary violence, at least in Western societies, is always the work of quite small, well-led minorities who in conditions of democracy are able to exercise for quite a long time a veritable tyranny over the people as a whole. Secondly, the privileged publicity which they invariably attract from the mass media, for reasons suggested at the beginning of this chapter, make them appear as the standard-bearers of liberty and progress. Consequently many people—who would not dream of indulging in such excesses themselves—simply because the protesters are young, liberal, radical or socialist in their group loyalties, instinctively support them against the establishment. Thus the polarization of opinion between Left and Right, authority and anti-authority, becomes more pronounced.

Conscience Silenced by Revolutionary Nationalism

It is when nationalist passions are identified with an insurrectionary movement that Christians are most prone to allow "the cause" to become the absolute determinant of conduct, excusing the total disregard of the Ten Commandments and all the precepts of Christian charity. Thus in Northern Ireland in the last three years the climate of violence has turned for the militant minorities into a kind of counter-religion; but for the peaceful majorities, both Protestant and Catholic, into an unending nightmare. The IRA, whose initiative started the urban guerrilla and developed the terrorist tactics of the revolutionary war, though almost all baptised Catholics, had for many years been frowned upon by the Irish bishops for the violence which caused them to be officially outlawed in the Republic itself. Yet, as the heirs of the traditional national revolt of the Irish against the English, they could always depend upon a certain fund of popular sympathy, not least among the American Irish. They have been responsible for the majority of killings both of unarmed civilians and of troops and police, largely by bombing. The Protestants, resentful at the loss of their political ascendancy and stung to revenge, produced a counter-terror in the form of the UDA and the Ulster Defence Volunteers. Protestant gunmen have been responsible for two thirds of those individual assassinations which are the chief horror of Belfast. Here then we have the worst fruits of revolution and counter-revolution practised in their most odious form by rival gangs of Christians. Needless to say, the IRA enjoys the unqualified support of the Soviet press, abundant arms from Eastern Europe, and the endorsement of revolutionary and liberation movements all over the world. The official branch of the organisation, now wholly Marxist, aims to establish revolutionary socialism throughout Ireland, South and North.

I include this brief account of a tragic, inconclusive conflict, the worst scandal in Christianity today, for it shows more poignantly than any theorising the dead end to which acceptance of the cult of violence leads. The churchmen, and particularly Cardinal Conway, the Primate of All Ireland, deserve every credit for their outright and unyielding condemnation of this flouting of the moral law and the Christian virtues. I have no doubt that though their authority is spurned by the gunmen, the silent majority of both Christian communities accept their judgment and share their yearning for peace. One of dozens of pronouncements by the Cardinal may be put on record here. It was made in December 1971. It is itself a sufficient answer to the political clerics who write *in vacuo* at a safe distance about the "theology of violence":

> The person who could shoot a man dead in his own sitting room, in front of his wife and children, is a monster. The person who could plant a bomb among innocent people is a foul murderer. The same thing can be said of the other horrible killings which have taken place during the past two weeks. Nothing can cloud our cold, clear condemnation of these deeds. To condone them in the slightest degree, even in thought, would be to become morally soiled oneself.

Chapter 3

THE MYTH
OF THE THIRD WORLD

The concept of the Third World plays a great part in the whole movement to direct the conscience of Christians into a revolutionary channel. Here, they are told, are two thirds of the human race living in a state of poverty and hunger while a minority of wealthy nations control the capital resources, the economic and monetary system, the prices of raw materials. Capitalism, mercantilism, imperialism, colonialism, neo-colonialism—all the abusive names, in other words, applied to the influence, past and present, of the civilised Western world in Africa, Asia and South America are invoked without discrimination to foist the guilt for this monstrous inequality upon Europeans (except of course Marxists). This picture of the world as divided between rich and poor is part of the truth—though the Communist empires of Russia and China are oddly enough excluded from the balance sheet; but it has been grossly oversimplified especially by the special pleading, exaggeration and distorted statistics of the Food and Agriculture Organisation of the United Nations for purposes of its own propaganda. This has been adopted in what we believe to be fallaciously generalised terms by those powerful elements in the Catholic Church whose aim is to turn the undoubted obligations of Christian charity into direct political action. This has made them easy game for the Communists whose exploitation of the grievances of the "colonial peoples" against "the imperialists" has for half a century been part of the whole strategy of the world revolution. Thus an anti-colonial, anti-white—and, incidentally, anti-American—sense is instinctively attached by generous and uncritical people to the very questionable proposition of the Roman Synod of Bishops in 1971 that "the struggle for justice clearly seems to be a constitutive dimension of the preaching of the Gospel, which is the mission of the Church for the redemption of humanity and its liberation from every oppressive situation." There is one great oppressive situation, we are given to believe; it is that of "the Third World."

Dom Helder Cámara, the eloquent Archbishop of Olinda and Recife in Brazil who has made himself the apostle of this view, had this to say recently to a meeting of members of both Houses of Parliament at Westminster:[11]

> Why do you not take concrete steps to bring about that economic independence which gives meaning to political independence? If not, the Third World will feel itself involved in a farce: we continue to be crushed by a neo-colonialism as oppressive and revolting as the old colonialism. Decades of development, one per cent of GNP for the poor nations, programmes of assistance —these cannot cover up the reality; the prosperity of the rich nations has as its price the proletarianisation and the ever increasing misery of the Third World. What is given with the right hand is incomparably less than what is taken away with the left. Even when capitalism is obliged, as it is today to grant political independence, it keeps nations under economic domination. They become the suppliers of raw materials: today they are usually industrialised with factories that carry a national label but which, in reality, are merely the playthings of great multinational corporations. . . .You are seeing an increasing radicalism take control of our earth. Why doesn't your political expertise help to show that the primary violence is the injustice that we see everywhere—which is not the monopoly of any one nation? Why don't you show that the reaction of the oppressed—or of young people in the name of the oppressed—is a secondary violence, itself followed by violence number three, the reaction of governments?

It is not clear what noble Lords and members of the House of Commons, or indeed any of us, are expected to do about all this. Is it Brazil, from which the orator comes, that he has in

---

11. June 27, 1972.

mind? His northeast corner of that country, with its large mix-
ture of Negroes in the population, is indeed desperately poor;
the conditions of life and unemployment are probably as bad
as anywhere in Latin America. But how can the well-intentioned foreigner intervene to help matters? Brazil is a great
and indeed prosperous country rightly jealous of its sovereignty and independence. The mitigation of the economic and
social evils of a section of its people can only be tackled by its
own authorities, as indeed they have been trying to do to no
inconsiderable extent for some time. No doubt what the Archbishop, like other radicals, dislikes most is the extent of United
States investments in Brazil. But it can equally be argued that
the "economic miracle" in progress in that country needs this
injection of foreign capital and technique. If, as is no doubt the
case, the resulting wealth is not equitably shared, the remedy
surely is a national responsibility.

If the Archbishop is chiefly concerned with former dependent territories which are now independent states, anyone who
is conversant with the problems of either public and private
aid or economic development must be aware of this same
sensitive national sovereignty, not to speak of the erratic policies of many of their rulers. There is nothing easy or uniform
about the ways in which the advanced industrial nations can
offer constructive cooperation to the less favoured in Africa,
Asia or Latin America. If political and economic independence
means, as this rhetoric seems to suggest, the absence of any
capital investment by companies and corporations and of
grants and loans from governments, that may well be the best
way to condemn them to perpetual poverty.

In fact all the generalisations in the typical quotation above
need to be taken apart and looked at—colonialism, neo-colonialism, capitalism, economic independence, etc. To begin with,
is there really such a thing as the "Third World?" It is in origin
a French journalistic cliché which religious and political do-
gooders have adopted for rhetorical purposes. Explains René
Coste[12]:

---

12. *Morale Internationale,* Desclée, 1964.

> The expression "Third World," is a recent creation. It was forged to designate the peoples (or the regions of the globe) which belong neither to the Western nor to the Communist blocs. Most of them have been under the political or at least the economic domination of the West. . . . Despite profound differences between them, which are not always on the wane, they are beginning to be conscious of their solidarity and their power. All are in fact underdeveloped peoples or countries. The analogy with the Third Estate of the Old Régime in France is evident. The nobility and the clergy were the two privileged orders, for historical reasons enjoying many privileges in public law. The mass of the population formed the Third Estate. Its most dynamic element, the cultivated bourgeoisie, aided indeed by members of the other orders, proceeded to struggle for the abolition of a situation which it considered anachronistic. So it made the Revolution. The Third World is the Third Estate of contemporary humanity.

The analogy is an arbitrary one if only because it is not evident which of the two Estates, the nobility or the clergy, we and the Communist powers are supposed to represent. But the notion is clear: those who are not classed as Worlds I and II are the underprivileged who will make the revolution.

It is a farrago of half truths. There is no uniformity in the countries thus lumped together as the Third World and few common features, except that food production per head has in fact risen more slowly in the "developing" than in the "developed" countries. Among the many states that do not belong to the two power blocs are such wealthy or potentially wealthy countries as Saudi Arabia, Kuwait and the other oil-rich sheikdoms of the Persian Gulf, Venezuela, Singapore, Malaysia, Mexico and the two giants of South America, Brazil and Argentina. If in such countries there are extreme contrasts of wealth and poverty the call is for vigorous social action to make proper use of the ample national resources available to redress these wrongs. Is it to this end that the Third World priests in Argentina seek to direct the aspirations of students and workers, or does not ideological agitation become an end in itself? And in what sense can Chile, a great country with its zinc, with its well-developed parliamentary system which a Marxist government was struggling to control, be described as part of this Third World?

Among the other Latin American states, there is indeed the almost ubiquitous problem of the rural Indian poor, and no one should minimise the great difficulties of governments, with the best will in the world, in raising their standard of life and improving agricultural production even with the wealth of minerals which several of these countries possess. It is here that resentment at the great United States corporations—some of it justified, some quite unreasonable—has become a major feature of nationalist politics, and it is in this region that the emotional anti-capitalist sentiments which inspire such orators as Dom Helder Cámara are most easily exploited by revolutionaries.

Certainly international economic advice and help should be available, such as the Economic Commission of the U.N. for Latin America provides. But the truth of the matter is that bad or inefficient government is the principal cause of economic disorder in most of these countries; and for this there is no external remedy.

In the Caribbean area there are the peculiar problems of making the best use of a bountiful soil and climate to sustain relatively dense populations which are the legacy of the era of Negro slavery. Here Cuba, from which there is a constant flow of dissatisfied emigrants, is hardly an advertisement for Marxist management of the basic sugar industry, though Cuba has certainly improved the housing of its people. As a centre from which revolutionary intrigues radiate, it has contributed nothing but mischief to the development of the South American continent. Haiti, the first independent Negro state, has an appalling history of misgovernment. For the rest, tourism covers a multitude of sins. But the political and economic conditions of all the Caribbean islands and litoral states are, on careful examination, quite different from one another. Few, given honest and efficient government, could not subsist satisfactorily on their own resources, though foreign capital and technique are desirable and in fact available to develop them, as in Guyana; though this aid is often frustrated by shortsighted nationalism. The natural markets for the products of the Lesser Antilles are mostly the European countries which used to govern them. This form of economic interdependence certainly needs constant adjustment. But to represent it as a form of organised economic oppression by the "developed countries" is pure fantasy.

The other main groups of countries supposedly included in the Third World are those of Southern Asia and Africa. Hence comes the Afro-Asian bloc with its dominating numerical position in the United Nations, steered by socialist propaganda in the early spate of anti-colonialism into a sterile posture of opposition to the West. But beneath the facade of this negative unity there are great distinctions.

India, the giant of southern Asia, has of necessity developed a form of politics all its own—and far different from Nehru's professions of pacifism and non-alignment. It courts Soviet support against China but depends a great deal upon American and Western European aid. Its parliamentary socialist government is the most successful of any of the former dependent countries, despite the ineradicable caste system, stubborn opposition to agrarian reforms and much corruption. Communal and national rivalries absorb more of the political concern of the Indian sub-continent—India, Pakistan and Bangladesh—than any of the supposed woes of Dom Helder Cámara's Third World, just as the internal conflicts between communism and opposing economic and religious forces hold the field in Ceylon, and tribal differences in Burma. In Bangladesh, where the great suffering in 1970–71 rightly aroused the pity of the whole world, what was the cause of it? In the first place an act of God, the appalling floods of the Ganges delta; next the mutual slaughter of Bengalis and Punjabs. In what conceivable sense were those "injustices" inflicted by imperialists or capitalists?

It is indeed in the teeming squalor of Calcutta and other great Indian cities that the most heartrending appeal is made to Christians in the Western world. Heartrending it is and ought to be. It has given rise to some heroic initiatives of Christian charity when, as in the rest of India, political conditions make it possible for private welfare organisations or experienced missionaries—constantly threatened with expulsion —to operate.

But what on earth has this to do with colonialism or neo-colonialism? The British Raj left, among other things, a legacy of law, military tradition, and civil service, without which the Indian administration could not function, and communications and irrigation which did much to diminish the recurrent famines. Since independence the United States has poured in wheat (much of it wasted). Various international consortia, the United Nations and divers governments have contributed to the development of new heavy industries. The Green Revolution has greatly increased agricultural production, especially of rice. But no governmental action, national or international, can alter the demographic trends of centuries or quickly remedy deeply rooted habits of the Hindu religion, the classes and the tribes. Caste and the sacred cow were not invented, *pace* Dom Cámara, by capitalism or neo-colonialism. Yet such are the basic impediments of this most important section of the Third World.

The economic and political situations of the African countries also suffer much stupid simplification. To begin with, all the former French, Belgian and Italian territories benefit through the Yaoundé Convention, periodically revised, from preferential import and export arrangements with the European Economic Community and also from credits, where needed, from its Bank. This in particular assures them a steady market for their primary products and a means of getting better prices for them. This privileged status is being extended, as the price of British entry into the Common Market, to former British dependencies in Africa as well as in the Caribbean, and to Mauritius, Fiji and other Pacific islands. This itself amounts to a vast mechanism of economic cooperation between Western Europe and (numerically) a majority of the countries conventionally classed as the Third World. But does any orator, ecclesiastical or otherwise, who dwells upon the woes of the Third World ever notice this important modern development? Of course not; because the whole of this moralising and emotional campaign is essentially political in purpose

35

and confined to the narrow simplifications of Marxist ideology. The object is not to evoke an accurate picture of the very varied economic situations of African countries but to produce a "revolutionary situation."

Objectively there is nothing in common between the countries of the Maghred and those of Black Africa south of the Sahara. The former comprise countries with a mix of revolutionary and conservative Arab nationalism and Islamic loyalties, and include two, Libya and Algeria, that are rich in petroleum and natural gas. South of the Sahara there are economically wealthy countries like the Ivory Coast, Kenya, Zaire and Zambia with its copper belt. Nigeria and Ghana were both left by the British with substantial financial reserves and a healthy balance of trade. Nigeria was brought low by an atrocious civil war from which it is now recovering; Ghana by the profligacy and megalomania of Nkrumah after which, following two coups d'état, it has nearly restored its solvency. The weakness of Senegal, as of Ghana (which the local government is seeking to remedy), is its too great reliance on a single crop (ground nuts; cocoa). All the Francophone states with the exception of Guinea receive and rely on more financial and technical aid from France (against which there is practically no antiimperialist feeling) than do the Anglophone states from Great Britain. Tanzania, committed to Mr. Nyerere's own brand of socialism and African nationalism, receives less advantage than, say, Kenya or Malawi from British and other foreign investment and aid. Uganda has ruined its trade through General Amin's inhuman expulsion of the Asian population. Ruanda has half destroyed its economy by atrocious tribal massacres. But it is the perennial disaster of drought in Africa which calls for humane assistance on the grand scale far more than any evil remotely connected with politics.

This is only a small sample of the distinctions which must be made between African states. The only characteristic that unites them, or rather their political intelligentsia, is the colour of their skin; the antipathy of black and brown to white is assumed and exaggerated out of all reason precisely by the Marxists and radicals, whose penetration of Christian civilisation we are studying and whose ideas have been exported to

36

Africa—in order to keep alive and stimulate, in the form of anticolonialism, resentment against European domination. There is in fact none of this European domination left (whatever its merits or demerits) except in the Portuguese provinces, whose peace, education, social and economic development and especially racial relations compare very favourably with conditions in any other countries of the continent; Rhodesia where white discriminatory rule is maintained with relative moderation; and the South African Republic where it is notoriously oppressive. (The Russian oppression of the conquered Baltic peoples is far worse, but somehow escapes the attention of our reformers.) Consequently the "liberation" of Southern Africa and Portuguese Guinea is the rallying cry which enables a belligerent spirit to be stirred up and sustained throughout independent Africa, though the majority of the Africans who give lip service to this cause have in fact no knowledge of or contact with these distant lands; and the rural guerrilla engaged for a decade in unsuccessful subversion against them is a small affair compared with the volume of words poured forth on the subject at the United Nations and Addis Ababa. Soviet and Chinese communism—the one mostly in the west, the other in the east of Africa—have had great success in securing control of the leading personnel of these "armies of liberation" whose armament comes almost solely from Communist sources, while their finances are mostly supplied nowadays by the Scandinavian Socialist parties, well-wishers in the United States, and that "Nonconformist conscience writ large," the World Council of Churches. While the support of most African governments for the "liberation" is more verbal than material, there are a few centres of violently aggressive revolutionary policy from which the wordy warfare is stimulated. Of these the most strident are the Republic of Guinea, in which an extreme version of Stalinist despotism is practised by the paranoiac Mr. Sekou Touré, Zanzibar, now incorporated in Tanzania, and Algeria, where many of the guerrillas have been trained. Logistically, all the "liberation" (or terrorist) raids into Angola are mounted from Zambia and Zaire; into Mozambique from Tanzania and Zambia; into Rhodesia and South Africa from Dar es Salaam and Zambia;

and into Portuguese Guinea from Conakry and Senegal. The monthly casualties caused by these operations, on one side and the other, are fortunately more a matter of dozens than of hundreds. They are nonetheless African lives which should be saved.

That, in broad outline, is the basis for the emotional appeal of the Third World with its revolutionary undertone, far more than the real and very diverse economic and social situations of the Asian, African and Latin American countries to which the term may be taken to apply. Of course there are poverty and hunger in many of these countries, lack of protein in the popular diet, tropical diseases. There always have been. While it is most desirable to raise a people's standard of living, it must be remembered that the types of food, health and housing by which international agencies appealing for support in the Western world often measure what they find in Indian villages or the African hinterland, are judged by the standards of Western, even of affluent nations. Yet neither a generation or two of European colonial rulers, nor the native politicians who in the last decade have followed them, have succeeded in their efforts to turn the people as a whole into artificial Europeans, even though the trappings of the European nation-state have been introduced. Throughout Black Africa, for instance, tribal loyalties and customs of great antiquity have proved much too deeply rooted to destroy. Further, the immensity of the land and in many cases the scattered population make penetration, whether of colonial or post-colonial administration, a very slow business. In areas of Central Africa, untouched by the relatively rare patches of industrialisation, subsistence farming of the simplest kind continues as it has for centuries—and not unhappily. Many admirable measures are being taken to teach better farming methods, and the long fight against diseases of man and beast continues. But even if efficient and disinterested government were the rule (which alas it is not), it would take a very long time to raise the material conditions of life to anything approaching the average in, say, the United States or England, France or Germany.

What is urgent, as Barbara Ward has brought out in her book

The Angry Seventies[13], is to try and arrest by some concerted measures the galloping urbanisation which, while it is a worrisome phenomenon of the affluent world, is having an even worse social effect in the so-called developing countries. With industries concentrating in and around a few cities—mostly seaport capitals in Africa—peasants are being drawn away from the land to form a rootless, de-tribalised proletariat as they are on an even greater scale in, say, Sao Paulo or Mexico City. What is needed is a well-planned series of labour-intensive projects based around small or medium-sized market and manufacturing towns. The question is whether there is any worldwide agency to bring this about. The author's confidence in action by the United Nations is alas not borne out by experience. It is a question of persuading and advising a host of individual governments and potential investors.

This is not the place to discuss policies of overseas development. I have drawn attention to these few facts only to show how wildly wide of the mark is the simple notion of rich countries giving money or food to poor countries. Further, even if it were true that the whole of the so-called Third World is in such a state of distress as speakers and writers like Dom Cámara suggest, which it is not, there is no truthful sense in which that condition can be called a collective injustice perpetrated by capitalism—that is, the economic system of the Western world. Revolutions may conceivably occur—there have been plenty of *coups d'état*—in this or that African, Asian or Latin American country. But the only form of revolutionary violence which has an international character in the context of the Third World and which colours the general agitation on this subject by Communist and Socialist parties and the Catholic Left, is the limited amount of subversion in Southern Africa which I have mentioned, along with occasional spasms in Latin America. There is thus no basis here for "a world revolution of the proletarian nations" which the Abbé Comblin imagines to

---

13. Pontifical Commission for Justice and Peace, Vatican City, 1971.

be inevitable. On what basis could they unite? Against whom could they rebel?

There is a more general fallacy underlying this apocalyptic rhetoric. Historically it is not the poor who make revolutions. Neither has any known revolution brought relief to the poor. Thus the Christian revolutionaries' habitual reference to the *Magnificat* and other Scriptural texts about bringing down the mighty from their seats and exalting the humble is nothing but a confidence trick. In reality it is simply a matter of substituting for existing rulers a group of professional revolutionary leaders who may be better or worse, but who are certainly not the poor. Hannah Arendt exposed this fallacy very aptly when she wrote:

> The rarity of slave rebellions and of uprisings among the disinherited and downtrodden is notorious; on the few occasions when they occurred it was precisely "mad fury" which turned dreams into nightmares for everybody. . . . To identify the national liberation movements with such outbursts is to prophesy their doom—quite apart from the fact that the unlikely victory would not result in changing the world (or the system) but only its personnel. To think finally that there is such a thing as a "Unity of the Third World" to which one could address the new slogan in the era of decolonisation, "Natives of all underdeveloped countries, unite!" (Sartre) is to repeat Marx's worst illusions on a greatly enlarged scale and with considerably less justification. The Third World is not a reality, but an ideology.[14]

---

14. *On Violence,* Allen Lane and The Penguin Press, 1970.

Chapter 4
POVERTY AND REVOLUTION

Hannah Arendt in the passage I have quoted puts her finger on the fallacy which underlies so much revolutionary rhetoric: the assumption that poverty and revolution are necessarily linked as cause and effect. It would be difficult to find any historical instance of a revolution started, still less carried through, by a mass of poor and hungry people, of whom there are indeed many in some countries of Latin America and southern Asia, and not a few also in depressed areas of the industrial countries today. What is true is that, at the other end of the social scale, the privileged class of nobility and landowners was the target—because of manifest injustice—of the great European revolutions, just as the holders of latifundia in parts of South America or millionaires who flaunt their wealth might well be today. Of course, the existence of genuine grievances for which there seems to be no peaceful or constitutional remedy can create a popular basis for insurrection. But in fact nearly every revolution, beginning with the French Revolution and going on to the Russian, has been the work of middle class intellectuals or professional politicians rousing the rural or urban poor by promises of better things in order to win the mass support they need to seize power. This is emphatically true of the professional revolutionaries, almost all ardent Communists, conducting today's "wars of liberation." The poor are the cannon fodder of the revolutionary. As for the professionals of the World Revolution, Tariq Ali, the Trotskyist militant who made his name in the student upheaval in England in the '60's, illustrates very well their relation to as well as their difference from the proletariat when he writes: "The ideas of the mass of the workers change only in the concrete process of the struggle itself. *Our* aim is therefore to win over as many workers as possible to the revolutionary movement."[15]

In some cases, as of genuine national insurrections against alien rule, rebellions have been evidently justified; in other cases not. In some they met with success; more often they ended only in bloody repression. But whatever the merits or demerits of the political programmes of the revolutionary leaders, it would be exceedingly difficult to prove that the poor —*Les Misérables* of Victor Hugo—derived any material or social benefits from a civil war (which is what revolution is), with all its hatred, violence and disruption of the existing framework of society, which they could *not* have had through a process of non-violent reform and economic progress. It took more than a generation before the standard of living in the Soviet Union reached anything approaching that of the workers in contemporary capitalist economies. Enforced collectivisation has never made a happy peasantry, not to mention the millions who were starved or killed in the process. The fact that, fifty-five years after the Revolution, Russia with half its population in agriculture could produce only 167 million tons of food-grain while six percent of the population of capitalist United States (even with one third of its grain land lying fallow) produced some 200 million tells its own story.

With these observations in mind we can see that there is nothing incompatible between the fervent and necessary appeals of the Second Vatican Council and the present Pope in his encyclical *Populorum Progressio,* for an immense effort of human solidarity and charity to help raise the whole standard and conditions of life of the poorer members of the family of nations, and the consistent condemnation by the papacy of revolutionary violence. The relevant passage of John XXIII's famous encyclical *Pacem in Terris* (161, 162) runs as follows:

> There are indeed generous souls who, when faced with a situation little or not at all consonant with justice, burn with desire

---

15. *The World and the School,* Atlantic Education Trust, November 1972.

to put everything right and are carried away by such ungovernable zeal that their reform becomes a sort of revolution.

To such people we would suggest that it is in the nature of things for growth to be gradual and that therefore in human institutions no improvement can be looked for which does not proceed step by step and from within. The point was well put by Our predecessor Pius XII: "Prosperity and progress lie not in completely overthrowing the old order but in well-planned progress. Uncontrolled passionate zeal always destroys everything and builds nothing. It inflames cupidity, never cools it. Since it does nothing but sew hatred and ruin, it drives men to the laborious undertaking of building anew on ruins left by discord the edifice which they started."[16]

Paul VI followed a similar line of thought in his encyclical *Populorum Progressio* (30, 31):

There are certainly situations where injustice cries to heaven. When whole populations destitute of necessities live in a state of dependence barring them from all initiative and responsibility, and all opportunity to advance culturally and share in social and political life, recourse to violence as a means to right these wrongs to human dignity is a grave temptation.

We know, however, that a revolutionary uprising, save when there is manifest, long-standing tyranny which would do great damage to fundamental personal rights and dangerous harm to the common good of the country, produces new injustices, throws more elements out of balance and brings new disasters. A real evil should not be fought against at the cost of greater misery.

The inconvenience of these pontifical generalisations is that it is tempting for the enemies of any social system or government to point to them and say, "*There* is the injustice which cries to heaven!" This is the invariable tactic of those, Christians included, who, true to the Marxist-Leninist dogma, apply this condemnation to the capitalist system as a whole. Since, however, the whole setting of the latter encyclical, to judge from its opening passages, seems to refer to the former colonial territories, it is a little difficult to pinpoint the countries in

---

16. Address to Italian Workers, 13 June 1943.

which these deplorable conditions exist. It is certainly not true of most of Africa except for the harsh racial discrimination of the South African Republic, the racial persecution of Asians in Uganda, and the political oppression of revolutionary Guinea to which I have referred, though millions live, as they always have, by subsistence agriculture. The poverty and squalor of some Indian cities might fit part of the description, though they cannot be applied to "whole populations." The nearest approach to it would seem to be the condition of the impoverished peasantry and urban slum-dwellers of certain Latin American countries, each with its own problems and responsibilities, despite the habit of making the United States the whipping boy for these defects.

But whatever may be said about the rhetorical style of both encyclicals, the practical and admirable object of which is to incite Christians and their governments in affluent countries to the maximum effort of generosity towards the poor and underdeveloped peoples, there is a most important aspect to these statements against revolutionary violence made by modern popes. It is that they are *not* "counter-revolutionary" in the sense of being condemnations of revolt against authority and the existing social order, such as were the declarations of the popes of the 18th and 19th centuries from Pius VI to Leo XIII —a tradition of the Church severely criticized by "theologians of revolution."[17] The argument, it will be observed, is that the existence of real injustices being assumed as well as the good intentions of the ardent reformer, revolution is shown to be the worst way to go about remedying it, because of the greater evils which it entails. Hence the emphasis of both *Pacem in Terris* and *Populorum Progressio* on constructive reforms to remove the causes of social disorder and to build a peaceful society in which everyone can, in the words of *Populorum Progressio,* "live a full human life, freed from servitude im-

---

17. "If we consider the history of the Catholic Church from 1789 to 1958 we find, in the words of the popes, the bishops, the clergy and Catholic publicists, so many condemnations of revolution—the French or Liberal Revolution first, then the Socialist Revolution—that one can speak of an almost unanimous concert. . . . All through the 19th century we can observe a faithful alliance between the Counter-Revolution and the Church." Comblin, *Théologie de la Révolution,* page 185.

posed on him by other men or by natural forces over which he has not sufficient control."

At the same time it is the emphasis of such pontifical statements on religio-political subjects which is important in assessing their practical effects upon opinion. It is undeniable that the emphasis of *Populorum Progressio* is on the woeful conditions of life in the developing (i.e., backward) countries of the non-Communist world:

> Today no one can be ignorant any longer of the fact that in whole continents countless men and women are tormented by hunger, countless numbers of children are undernourished so that many of them die in infancy, while the physical growth and mental development of many others are retarded and, as a result, whole regions are condemned to the most depressing despondency.

Yet as against this surely overdrawn picture, there is no mention in the document of the suppression of religious and political liberty, not to speak of the liquidation of whole classes of human beings, in the vast areas dominated by Communist Russia and China; hardly any regard for the very considerable volume of aid given by the Western powers to individual Asian, African and Latin American countries—insufficient, no doubt, by the highest standards of human solidarity but unprecedented in history; no reference in the short passage about revolution, quoted above, to the duty of obeying duly constituted authority as the normal requirement of civil society (which the Vatican Council recognized in this connection[18]). It was inevitable therefore that this important document, so lavishly praised by official Soviet propagandists such as Professor N.A. Kowalski of the Soviet UNESCO Commission and Dr. A. Polyanov, the Deputy Editor of *Izvestia,* should be taken by Marxists as confirmation of their new thesis that the Church can be a useful ally in promoting the world revolution ("the victory of socialism"). As *La Pasionaria,* the famous demagogue of the Spanish Civil War, said at the Congress of the Rumanian Communist Party at Karlovy-Bara in 1972,

---

18. See page 13.

45

"The Catholic religion instead of being an opiate is in the process of becoming a leaven."[19] Nor is it surprising that the Catholic Justice and Peace Commission, whose establishment was announced in the encyclical, should have been steered so soon into equating the Injustice (with a capital I) and tyranny from which it is morally right to "liberate" people, by violence if necessary, with capitalism, imperialism, colonialism and all the other ill-defined bogeys of the Left.

It would indeed be untrue and unfair to take this evidence of Pope Paul's anguished concern for the poor and needy out of the whole context of the Church's social teaching about the proper ordering of human society in accordance with the natural law, the goal of national and international peace, the subordination of all efforts to better the material conditions of men to their supernatural end, and in particular man's dependence upon the Commandments and the love of God. It may well be that the widespread tendency, especially among the younger priests of South America, to justify revolution by exploiting the Church's novel emphasis upon the duty to relieve material suffering, hunger and social depression has led the Pope on subsequent occasions to be more outspoken and unqualified in his condemnation of violence. Thus in the course of his visit to the Conference of Latin American Bishops in Colombia in 1968 he said to a great meeting of peasants at Mosquera:

> Finally we exhort you not to put your trust in violence and revolution. It is contrary to the Christian spirit, and it can also retard instead of helping forward that social betterment to which you have every right to aspire.

In his sermon at Mass the same day and in his discourse to the assembled bishops he emphasized the same theme; and it is one he has returned to several times in the years following. Thus, when he welcomed British Prime Minister Heath at the Vatican in October 1972, he spoke of his "prayerful hope that peace and justice may soon be established in Northern Ireland" and added that "violence, wherever it may manifest

---

19. Quoted in *Force et Violence*, Actes du Congrès de Lausanne, VII, 1972.

itself and in whatever form, should be rejected and condemned."[20]

For those, then, who take seriously their loyalty to the Vicar of Christ, there can be no question that revolution and the violence which it inevitably entails are not the way to promote justice and peace. They are irrelevant to the relief of poverty and hunger and all those works of social charity for which the Pope has done so much to arouse the conscience of Christians and other men of goodwill.

---

20. See also page 105.

Part Two

THE THEOLOGY
OF REVOLUTION
EXAMINED

Chapter 5
THE THESIS

Theology in the proper sense of the word is the science of the divine, the study of the attributes of Almighty God, his Law and his Revelation. It has, however, become a deplorable habit to attach the name of theology to any study of particular aspects of human nature which involve moral problems. Thus we have "political theology," the "theology of woman," "the theology of liberation," "the theology of labour," and what not. But, whereas in the case of most of these phrases all that is really meant is the ethics of certain human relations, there is something to be said for the title Theology of Revolution which has been taken for their works by writers such as Richard Shaull, the Abbé Joseph Comblin and the German Evangelicals who in the last ten years have devoted themselves to arguing the case for committing the Church to political revolution. For it is the whole of natural and revealed religion, including the significance of the life and teaching of Jesus Christ, which is involved in their arguments. The emergence of this singular phenomenon is, as we have noticed, of very recent origin. In fact, it can be attributed to just a few fairly well-defined political forces which have been at work since the early 1960's. These we shall study in another chapter; but before doing so, it is necessary to have as fair a picture as possible of the actual tenets of this new religion for, mistaken as I believe it to be, there is no doubting the sincerity and fervour of its advocates.

Protestant Revolutionary Ideas

The ideas of some of the leading Protestant authors concerned are summarised by Dr. René Padilla, Associate General Secretary for Latin America of the International Fellowship of Evangelical Students in *Is Revolution Change?*[21], a valuable critique of the whole subject by a group of Evangelical writers:

> To them revolutions are nothing less than the means through which God is carrying out His purpose in history. God's action is of a political nature—it is orientated towards the transformation of social structures. Harvey Cox[22] says that God is present above all in political events, in revolutions, in revolts, in invasions, in defeats. God not only permits or desires change but He carries it out, and He does this through revolutions. Richard Shaull, in agreement with Paul Lehmann, maintains that "revolution must be understood theologically, for it is set firmly in the context of God's humanizing activity in history. As a political form of change, revolution represents the cutting edge of humanisation."[23] He believes that the presence and power of God in the renovation of life are manifested above all wherever there is a struggle to make human life more human "on the frontiers of change where the old order is passing away and the new order is coming into being in the world.[24]
>
> "In the light of this concept of revolution, the responsibility of the Christian is obvious—to be present in the revolution." And Dr. Padilla further quotes Shaull as writing, "Our task is not to impose certain values, but rather to recognize and live according to those that hold sway in the world; it is not to give meaning to life but rather to discover the meaning that life has in the world that participates in redemption; not to establish order in the universe, but rather to share in the new order of things that is taking shape through social transformation."[25]

21. Inter-Varsity Press, London, 1972.

22. *The Church and Revolution.* World Council of Churches; Association Press, New York 1967.

23. *Revolutionary Change in Theological Perspective* in *Christian Social Ethics in a Changing World,* World Council of Churches; Association Press, New York, 1966.

24. *Christianity and World Revolution,* Harper, New York, 1963.

25. *Y un Dios que actua y transforma in historia,* America Hoy, I.S.A.L., Montevideo, 1966.

Dr. Padilla's judgment of this extraordinary abdication of Christian principle in favour of the acceptance of temporal phenomena, which the Conference on Church and Society, held at Geneva in 1966, made its own, is equally applicable to the Catholic apologists of revolution. Referring to "the widespread hope outside the Western world, that, on the basis of a supposed dialectic of history, revolution will create the new society that the majority desire," Dr. Padilla says:

> The "theology of revolution" takes upon itself to provide theological justification for this hope. All its errors stem from the fact that it takes as its starting point the revolutionary situation and interprets Scripture on the basis of presuppositions derived from Leftist ideologies. Instead of showing the relevance of revelation to revolution, it makes revolution its source of revelation. The result is a secular gospel whose dominant emphases parallel those of Marxism.[25A]

The most comprehensive exposition of the subject by a Catholic author, to judge from the impressive bibliography, seems to be Father Joseph Comblin's *Théologie de la Révolution,* to which we have already referred. It is no surprise that, like, the Protestant Richard Shaull who spent ten years in Brazil and ten in Colombia, he also has a background of Latin American pastoral experience, in Chile and Brazil, since 1958.

The Revolutionary Themes of Christianity

The section of his book in which he appears to put forward most clearly his own conclusions is entitled "The Revolutionary Themes of Christianity." These he summarizes under thirteen headings: The New World, The Promise, Hope, Liberty, The Covenant [*l'Alliance*], The Spirit, The Judgment of God, The Kingdom of God, Conversion, Charity, The Party of the Poor, Death and Resurrection, and The True Image [*Figure*] of the Church. Here, translated from the French, are the main points of each.

25A. *Is Revolution Change?*

The New World

"Behold I make all things new" (Apoc. XXI, 5). The forecast of newness is a dominant feature of Messianism in the Old Testament. The New Testament corresponds to the prophecies. It proclaims the coming of the New Man, the new people, the new Covenant, the new birth, the new Jerusalem.

The 2nd Vatican Council, speaking of a new heaven and a new earth, says (*Gaudium et Spes*, 39): "The expectation of a new earth must not weaken but rather stimulate our concern for cultivating this one. For here grows the body of a new human family, a body which even now is able to give some kind of foreshadowing of the new age."

Conclusion

"The newness of Christ is . . . a continuing movement of 'transcendence' towards the future. Compare this concept of newness with that of the Revolution; the design [*dessein*] is exactly the same. If the two are not united, it is perhaps that the practical application is different. But it can be different and yet allow a partial coincidence."

The Promise

This theme is correlative to that of newness. "The Christian existence means living the promises of Christ. The promise necessarily uses the language of Utopia; it is Utopia made possible. . . . The Revolution also speaks the language of Utopia. The question is: Is there a connection between the promises of Christ, the apocalyptic promises, and the promises in which the revolutionaries believe? Many mediaeval heresies made that connection. Engels himself saw in apocalypsism an affinity with the social revolution. They may have been mistaken about the speed of applying the promises, but were they mistaken on the basic question? There may perfectly well be a partial coincidence between the promise of the Gospel and the revolutionary Utopia."

Hope

"For the Christian, to hope is always to believe in the impossible. . . . Vatican II seemed impossible. . . . It was necessary to seize the occasion to produce a new image of the Church. The Council was alive in the form of hope for nearly a century, at least in the minds of some individuals who believed in the impossible. . . .

"The forces which create new forms of society are latent, but can only come into operation in certain circumstances if they can be manipulated by minorities who live by hope. . . .

"Christianity is indifferent to the choice of persons who hold power or to the form of government, but not to the structure of society. It destroys the foundations of closed societies and only accepts societies which are open to the future and which live by hope. This is how one can see Christianity and Revolution in the same setting *(sur le même plan)*."

Liberty

"The affirmations of the Prophets in the face of the powers and dominations of their day show the foundation of liberty, the fundamental attribute of man according to the anthropology of the Bible. The New Testament is even clearer. The struggle of Jesus against the Pharisees was a vindication of liberty. Jesus was condemned to death because he wanted to replace a religion of servitude and observances by a religion of love. The Sermon on the Mount is the Christians' charter of liberty. . . . In St. John's Gospel Jesus proclaims, 'The truth shall make you free . . .'

"Ecclesiastical institutions are not always to be found on the side of those who achieve liberty, but sometimes on the side of those who impede it. What matter? Christianity is not the monopoly of ecclesiastical institutions. It is the Christian people that is at work. It is not surprising that 'heretics' have very often proclaimed the message of liberty with more fervour than the orthodox. But this does not destroy the Bible message. . . . One can well admit that revolutionary liberty does not express all that is comprised in the concept of Christian liberty. But is there not at least a partial coincidence between them?"

The Covenant [l'Alliance]

"What makes the People of God is the Covenant. . . . The people of the Covenant means that the rule of necessity has been replaced by the rule of liberty, in the language of Marx which is indeed the language of the Bible. It is not blood, or land, or history, or geography but a common vocation that unites them . . . Their bond of association is their common pursuit of the future which God makes for them; that is their liberty.

"Now we find this idea of the Covenant exactly in the principle of the mediaeval Commune, which is the peak of the first great European revolution. It corresponds to the 'Covenant' of the Puritans, the foundation, in the American sense, of the nation. It is basically what the Social Contract of Jean Jacques Rousseau means. . . .

"When John XXIII refers to justice and peace, love and truth, in the context of the social problems of our time he is uttering a Messianic message *(il fait du messianisme)*, he is proclaiming a temporal realisation of the Messianic prophesies . . . and placing himself in line with the revolutionary project of all Christian history. Here again there can be a partial coincidence between the concept of the Covenant and the revolutionary project of the human community which the Revolution claims to establish."

The Spirit

In this section the author is clearly inspired by the notion of the Church of the Spirit *versus* the institutional Church, which is one of the characteristics of the New Theology. He makes much of the teaching, officially condemned, of Father Joachim de Flore in the 12th century concerning the development of the spiritual Church. He goes on to claim that "Franciscanism is a first example of applying the action of the Spirit to history in the concrete. . . .

"One may well think that, after making so many concessions to paganism for the sake of being embodied in history, the Christian people is seeking to free itself from that cloak in order to conform more closely to its essential character. And why should that effort be confined to the purely ecclesiastical sphere and not affect the economic, social and political structures within which Christians live?"

The Judgment of God

"The vision which Christianity gives us of the new world is not that of organic growth or quantitative development. It is the vision of a drama and a struggle. The old man must be destroyed so that the new man may be born . . ."

The judgment of God is an exhortation to conversion. His judgment on the things of this world is announced in order that men may be converted so as not to suffer that judgment. That is the meaning of prophecy. When the popes publish social encyclicals, they exercise a prophetic role.

"It is true that this prophecy does not seem to be revolutionary. In fact its interpreters are scared when the revolutionary implications of their oracles emerge. Yet, when the popes publish encyclicals like *Pacem in Terris* or *Populorum Progressio*, who cannot see that the demands which they make cannot begin to be met except by means of a revolution? What *Populorum Progressio* requires, both at the national and at the international level, is a total subversion of the established order and a radical change in the most fundamental principles of contemporary society. If this kind of prophecy perseveres to its logical conclusion, it cannot fail to inspire a revolution."

The Kingdom of God

Oddly enough the author in a short discussion of the kingdom does not quote the Lord's own prayer, "Thy kingdom come, thy will be done on earth as it is in heaven." He writes that "the reign of God means that God overcomes His adversaries, liberates and saves His people. . . . God does not establish a kingdom in this world. But He acts . . . He makes his intention prevail by acts which change the course of human affairs. . . .

"One cannot say that a revolution will ever be able to install a 'kingdom of God' among men, but one can recognize in the march of liberty the action of God which conquers evil, servitude and idolatry."

Conversion

"Jesus said, 'Do penance, for the kingdom of God is at hand' (Matthew 4.17).

"When the prophets preach conversion to justice, they demand that justice be practised in the concrete in social relations. It is in this sense that we must understand conversion today: conversion is a change in social attitudes. But if social attitudes are determined by the framework and structures of society, how can conversion be real unless it changes these structures themselves? That is how today's theologians place revolutionary action in the line of conversion."

Charity

Recalling Thomas Münzer's denunciation of "faith without works" in his celebrated polemic against Luther, Father Comblin writes:

"He identified Luther's counter-revolutionary attitude, in the revolution called in history the Peasants' War, to the doctrine of faith without works. Indeed it seems that not only in the case of Luther but all through the 'Protestant era'—and Catholicism also had its 'Protestant era'—insistence upon the purely interior character of faith encouraged Christians to be indifferent to the social and political situations which were destined to provoke the great revolutions of modern times.

"What matters is our conception of love. The bourgeoisie only give it a sentimental meaning. They cultivate it in private life, but exclude it in social life. They think only of philanthropy and almsgiving . . . The same problem arises in aid to underdeveloped countries.

"Almsgiving establishes an attitude of fundamental inequality between giver and receiver . . . Charity, to show real respect of one's neighbour, must try to suppress the situation which makes almsgiving necessary. It puts the initiative into the hands of the poor and the oppressed. Which amounts to saying that it places itself at the service of the Revolution."

The Party of the Poor

A manifesto of fifteen bishops of the Third World is quoted: "Christians and their pastors must recognize the hand of Almighty God in the events which periodically depose the powerful from their seats and raise up the humble, send the rich empty away and satisfy the poor.

"In this text," comments the author, "the words of the *Magnificat* are applied to the revolution." (On this, see Chapter 4.)

"In fact the Gospel, while it is addressed to all men, has not the same message for all: to the poor it announces liberation and to the rich the deprivation of their riches. The two messages are complementary. . . . In a sense the Gospel seems to demand a kind of 'voluntary revolution.' What relation has this to what one calls *the* Revolution? One can neither identify the two, nor distinguish them totally."

Death and Resurrection

"The mystery of the Cross is at the centre of Christianity. The problem is to know whether it must only be lived within the interior life of the person or whether it does not also characterize social and historic life. This latter point of view . . . is considered more and more seriously in the perspective of the new 'political theology.'

"Death and resurrection: death is the judgment of God, conversion the fall of the rich, the end of the old world. Resurrection is the victory of God, the triumph of the poor, the achievement of the promises, hope, charity in action, the liberty of the children of God, the new people of the covenant in peace and justice."

The True Image [Figure] of the Church

"The Church to-day is in search of its role in the midst of the world. . . . The theology of revolution places the Church beyond its present structures. In this way it makes it even more acceptable. The Church must not be identified with what it actually is, but with what it will be. . . .

"The traditional Church has a psychology which is accustomed to a majority situation. Traditional Christians dislike a minority condition. The clergy like it even less. To make it comprehensible and acceptable, the theology of revolution offers the role of being an active and revolutionary leaven."

Conclusion

"If we bring together all the themes we have considered, it is undeniable that they make a coherent picture. It amounts to a synthesis of Christianity to which we have not been accustomed by our traditional catechisms and manuals of theology. But the synthesis undoubtedly corresponds to the structure of the Christian message. . . . What name are we to give it? If we search the vocabulary of contemporary culture we shall find no other name for it but Revolution. No doubt we do not find in the concept of Revolution all the elements of our message. But in the thought of the present day there is no other concept which fits it better."

The author whom we are considering, having established, as he believes, the essentially revolutionary character of the Christian message, proceeds to the question of whether there is a concrete connection between "Biblical revolution" and revolutionary action today. To find an answer he gives his own version of the life of Jesus—or rather of certain selected aspects of his life and death. He dismisses a recent accusation that "the theologies of violence lack evangelical roots and spiritual sobriety"[26] by saying:

---

26. M. J. Guillou, O. Clément and J. Bosc, *Evangile et Révolution*, Le Centurion, Paris, 1968.

> This argument is repeated incessantly: Jesus did not engage in politics. Jesus did not make a revolution. Jesus did not accept the function of the temporal Messiah, such as the crowds wanted to impose upon him. Jesus remained indifferent to the Zealots' movement of violent resistance, etc. Broadly speaking [*en gros*] all this is undeniable. At least if we go no further than noting this: Jesus did not want to use violence himself and did not wish his disciples to have recourse to violence. If we go beyond that simple statement, everything becomes less clear.

It is chiefly by his presentation of four aspects of the public life and death of Jesus that the author seeks to establish his thesis that the Christian call to revolutionary action is consistent with the Gospels:

1) Jesus was a Jew and all his acts were necessarily grounded in the history of Israel. Consequently he was "first of all a rebel against the whole pagan universe." Instead, however, of confining the revolt as did the Pharisees to living as a sect separated from the rest of the world, he launched this Jewish revolt (through his apostles) amidst the pagans. He could have had no illusions about the resistance which the Bible message would provoke in the pagan world. Thus "it must be recognized that the attitude of Jesus is fundamentally revolutionary. To throw men formed in the Old Testament world into the midst of pagan society is to cause fermentation, shock and revolution. At the least, it means planting in the heart of the Roman world a principle of permanent confrontation."

2) Jesus cultivated the poor and sought his adherents among them. "It is not from sentimentality or 'populism' that Jesus, himself a simple artisan, formed his church with simple people. It was political realism. . . . The great men of Israel never did the slightest damage to the forces of the Empire . . . Only the poor could mix with the poor of the Empire. But the poor of Jesus were no slaves (slaves never make a successful revolution), but the sons of those Hebrews who had established a Covenant *(Alliance)* in Sinai, who had laws of justice and felt themselves all free and equal. To send these poor Israelites into the pagan world, reaffirming their spiritual identity and their continuity while preventing them from isolating them-

61

selves and living on their own, amounted to launching in the world the ferment of revolutions. How could Jesus not have known and wished that, at least confusedly?"

3) "Jesus aroused messianic hopes. Though he refused to assume a messianic role himself . . . we believe that he well knew the kind of reactions which his mode of speaking and acting would provoke. If he aroused messianic hopes of justice and peace in this world, it was because this had a meaning in his plan. Otherwise he could very well have done without it and so avoided confusion. If he had only wanted to arouse the desire for heaven, he would have kept to the tradition of *sapientia* [*la tradition sapientielle*] and quoted only authors who had treated that subject."

4) "The problem of the death of Jesus is that it would have been so easy to avoid it. Why go to Jerusalem, defy all the authorities of Israel and confirm all the suspicions of the Romans?" Here our author, concerned with the facts of political history, makes a particularly offensive reference to the doctrine of the Atonement when he writes: "To fashion a pious picture of Jesus *(pour l'iconisation de Jésus)* is no problem. Jesus went up to Jerusalem because he had to die, and he had to die in order to expiate the sins of men. Everything was worked by the hand of God. Pilate, the Pharisees and Jesus are only marionettes who perform what was written by the prophets. . . . If, on the contrary, we wish to find the human aspect of Jesus' death, we can explain it as follows from its observable historical results.

"The death of Jesus created an impassable gulf between official Judaism and his disciples. . . . It excommunicated them and made them rejected by the old Israel. In face of this challenge, they had to take their courage in their hands." Free from all links with the past they plunged into the pagan world. "It was the open door toward a new future for a new Israel." St. Paul (Ephesians II, 15, 16) is quoted as describing the situation in its historic and political sense.

"Such a death is explained, humanly speaking, in terms of a plan to create an irreparable rupture in Israel in order to compel the Christians to go and confront the Roman Empire outside the narrow walls of that fortress which is the Israel of the Old Testament.

"Further, Jesus' witness before the Roman authorities shows a new way of confronting the Empire. There can no longer be a hidden life, lived on the periphery of great events. Jesus affronted the representative of the Emperor. His disciples were to feel invited to do likewise."

The particular political selections, omissions and interpretations of Christian themes and of certain aspects of the life and death of Jesus Christ, illustrated by the above quotations, may seem a little remote from the revolutionary demonstrations and actions, subversions and wars which this school of churchmen excuse and justify at the present time. On the contrary, we find in the slant which is thus given to the Christian message itself the most serious and indeed dangerous contribution which the "theology of revolution" is making to contemporary politics. From the closely reasoned passages of *Théologie de la Révolution* in which the author seeks to draw practical conclusions from his interpretation of the Bible, the following three extracts are significant:

1) *The Inevitability of the Revolution*

Everything points to the fact that we are now faced with a new episode in the revolution of the West. . . . "What must we do?" is the all-important question. In any case one cannot remain not doing anything to make this message of the Bible incarnate in life. No doubt we shall be asked, "Why revolution and not some other course of action?" Why must social action necessarily take the form of the revolutionary movement and nothing else? The answer is clear; there *is* nothing else. Over twenty centuries, nothing else has been invented. So long as the West is the West, there is little likelihood of finding anything else. In the historic situation in which we are placed, there is no alternative [*il n'y a rien d'autre qui se présente*].

Kismet. It is bound to happen. It is this fatalism, closely akin to Marxist determinism, which has such a baneful attraction for a generation which has lost its moral and intellectual roots and is looking around for an answer. We shall return later to the many fallacies in this statement.

2) *Sin and Suffering Dismissed as Irrelevant*

> Every revolution has its detritus—disorders, folly, useless destruction, deformation and corruption of every kind. That is characteristic of any collective action. But we must not fail to see the woods for the trees. It is necessary to make a global comparison of epochs. Nobody in the West wants to return to Byzantinism or to the aristocratic, despotic and clerical rule of the Ancien Régime. This shows that the revolutions essentially attained their objectives, however limited those objectives in respect to the totality of human needs.

In other words, the end justifies the means. Let Revolution roll on! There is no regard for the rights of the person, the lives of the innocent, the safety of the home and all the requirements of natural law and morality which it is the purpose of civil society to safeguard; all those things, in fact, which the traditional moralist would say must be weighed in the balance against initiating violent insurrection, except in the case of grave and manifest oppression.

3) *Christianity and Marxism*

The evolution of official Catholic teaching is traced historically in *Théologie de la Révolution* from the downright condemnation of socialism, communism, and nihilism by Leo XIII to the tendency to encourage dialogue and practical cooperation between Christians and Marxists which found its way into one passage (No. 21) of the Constitution *Gaudium et Spes* of the Vatican Council.[27] We must examine also the practical consequences of that evolution, which are doubtfully edifying. We may note, however, how this author answers what he calls "the conservative and basically counter-revolutionary thesis"

---

27. "While rejecting atheism root and branch, the Church sincerely professes that all men, believers and unbelievers alike, ought to work for the rightful betterment of this world in which all alike live."

that atheism impregnates all the elements of Marxism and consequently "he who refuses to accept atheism must also eschew Marxism as a whole. . . ."

Against this the revolutionary thesis is that there is no indissoluble link in Marxism between atheism and the philosophy of revolution, and that one can accept one without the other. Consequently, provided a way could be found to re-frame the system while keeping its essential elements, one could reconcile Marxism and Christianity. The problem would not be more difficult to resolve than that of reconciling Aristotelianism and Christianity which was solved in the Middle Ages. Everyone agrees that the achievement of St Thomas Aquinas was more than an easy concordance, more than an opportunist facade of a solution; but rather a real integration of Aristotelianism. Cannot one envisage something similar—*mutatis mutandis*—with Marxism?

Upon which one might observe: where there's a will, there's a way.

Chapter 6
WHAT IS THE REVOLUTION?

The eloquent elaboration of the case for identifying Christianity with the revolutionary movement, which we have seen in the last chapter, differs from the Protestant development of the argument (e.g., in the documents of the Geneva Conference of 1966 on the *Church and Society* and of the Uppsala Assembly of the World Council of Churches in 1968) chiefly in not being so much preoccupied with conditions in underdeveloped countries and Latin America in particular. It will be more appropriate to examine the latter when we come to discern the political forces which have produced in the last decade the extraordinary phenomenon of the Christian revolutionary campaign. The Abbé Comblin's thesis, however, about the revolutionary themes of Christianity and the example of Jesus Christ himself goes back, as it were, to first principles and evolves a theory which claims universal application, not without allusions to and criticisms of papal utterances on social questions from age to age, which Protestant apologists for or opponents of revolution usually ignore.

It is this general thesis therefore which we propose to analyse critically under three heads. First, what *is* the Revolution, which is nowhere clearly defined but with which the various imperatives and trends of the Christian message are said to coincide, and which is supposed to have characterized the history of European civilization? Secondly, what *is* this Christianity which is presented to us? Do the selected Biblical texts and themes give a full and fair picture of the teaching of Christ or not? Thirdly, what are historically the political events and developments of recent years which have produced this cult of revolution in the Church?

Let us start in this chapter with the Revolution.

The Mood of Revolution

What *is* the Revolution at which every knee should bow? Books pour from the presses nowadays on violence and revolution. To be revolutionary has become all the fashion with the progressives, politicians, publicists, journalists, radio commentators, university dons, priests, students and schoolmasters. Some of what is being published is, of course, of scientific worth, examining the origin and character of various revolutions which have taken place and their consequences—which more often than not have resulted in the revolution of yesterday becoming the conservatism of tomorrow. But the popular revolutionary mood now is more a matter of sentiment than of science or political theory. It is a general disposition to question and defy authority, evidence of that crisis of authority which afflicts Church and State and all forms of organised society in the Western world today. The fanatical militant, at different levels, takes advantage of this mood to produce university disorders, street demonstrations, scuffles with the police, wildcat strikes and picketing which are the joy of television but which have not so far been more than pinpricks in the pachyderm of the modern industrial state. What indeed is more serious is the effective exploitation by able Communist leaders of the solidarity of the great trade unions in Western democratic countries such as Great Britain and Italy, in order to paralyse communications and other essential services—a process which exalts collective selfishness against the common good. But this form of economic subversion, invariably supported by left-wing intellectuals, has not so far approached a revolution in the proper sense. Meanwhile revolts against existing authority all over the world, however divers their character, exert a fascination upon progressive opinion in the West and are assured of sympathetic treatment in the mass media.

An able English historian[28] describes this phenomenon as follows:-

> Every time a new group of Arab colonels rolls their tank regiments into Damascus or Baghdad and shoots their predecessors, with or without benefit of so-called judicial process, a new "revolutionary" movement has attained instant existence. And the world is full of revolutionary movements, whose members often live high on the international hog, trundling between congresses and training courses from Havana to Moscow and from Cairo to Peking, with the inevitable parade of photogenic damsels in fetching uniforms carrying machine pistols across their arm for peace and the revolution against imperialism. Revolution is the great romanticism, inspiring dull Scandinavian Social Democrats to send arms to the thoroughly *élitist* and undemocratic IRA and staid Churchmen to vote money to support inter-tribal warfare in Central Africa.
>
> As an ultimate form of lunacy it can inspire the Weathermen to blow themselves up or a Baader-Meinhof gang to attack the very people they have come to "liberate." Revolutions, *pronunciamentos, coups d'état,* all are lumped together, confused in a warm-hearted welter of mawkish sentimentality, of affected humanitarianism which will nevertheless condone cruelty and social disruption on the widest scale. One cannot, they will say, as did the generals of 1914–18, make an omelette without breaking eggs. The historian, however, has to ask whether the omelette ever made its appearance.

It is difficult to absolve the earnest Christian authors whom we have quoted from the charge of being carried away by this prevalent emotional urge and of jumping on the revolutionary bandwagon. Once they abandon the practical examination of the case for or against rebellion in particular times, places and circumstances—which, as we have shown, is the only rational way of determining the right or wrong of the use of force in civil society—for the commitment to revolution as a kind of permanent religion, which is what their thesis amounts to,

---

28. D.S. Watt, Reader in International History, University of London, in *The World and the School*, Sept. 1972.

they sacrifice intellect to emotion, fact to feeling, and are bound to twist history to their purpose. It is really no use speaking about the Christian call to newness of life, to covenant or promise, or about the prophetic denunciation of the rich having the same sort of *design* or purpose as the Revolution, without telling us what exactly is the positive end or better ordering of society which the Revolution is intended to achieve, and how. What is not difficult—and it informs almost all the instances given in *Théologie de la Révolution,* in Richard Shaull's works, and in moving accounts of the economic troubles of the Third World—is to describe what has been or is deplorable, evil, unjust, oppressive in human persons and institutions or the perennial contrast between the rich and the poor, the powerful and the weak at various stages of the human story. Unquestionably there has always been an obligation of natural justice and charity, powerfully reinforced by the true Christian spirit, to right these wrongs; but what is there to prove that political *revolution,* though justified in certain extreme cases, has ever been the normal, or the best, still less the divinely intended method to right them? How often has the liberty, invariably promised by the revolutionary leaders, ever been really attained at the personal level, except for the members of the victorious party, class or government, from the Reformation of the 16th century through the French Revolution and its sequels in Spanish America, to the Russian Revolution and its sequels in this century? Genuine national risings against foreign rule have indeed sometimes, though not always, been the exception, resulting in a widely felt sense of political freedom. But, if we take the worst form of oppression of man by man, the institution of slavery, it was not by any political revolution that it was ended but by the slow and very chequered progress of the Christian spirit between the 4th century A.D. and the 1860's.

The Real World Revolution

But, whatever judgment the historian may make about the merits or demerits of past revolutions, the Revolution which the Theologians of Revolution are seeking to identify with the

Christian Church can only be the Revolution as it exists and is developing in the world today. Here we can distinguish between the general revolutionary effervescence, to which I allude at the beginning of this chapter, and *the* World Revolution of Marx and Lenin, complete with its dogmas and formulas for power, of which Moscow and Peking are the rival oracles. It is the latter which has held the field since 1917; and, however much the Trotskyite may denounce Leninist tactics or the Marcusian preach freedom from all established systems and standards or the New Left pursue violent revolt regardless of strategy, they would almost certainly not exist were it not for the Russian Revolution. They all share the following basic features: 1) belief in the *inevitability* of World Revolution in the sense of the disintegration or overthrow of the existing social and economic order; 2) belief in the ultimate triumph of the working class and the extinction of other classes; 3) denial of God and an objective moral law; 4) denial of the spiritual and intellectual liberty of the person; 5) denial of the personal right to property; 6) opposition to all authority other than that based on the supposed interests of the working class, as interpreted by the revolutionary party. Lenin's assimilation of the peoples of the colonial or ex-colonial territories in their struggle against "the imperialists" to the working class in its classic Marxist antagonism to the bourgeoisie, is also now an article of faith of all revolutionary groups, lively as is the controversy between those who, like Frantz Fanon, see the *Lumpenproletariat* of the Third World as the great hope of socialist revolution, and the orthodox Marxist[29] for whom the working class (little as it resembles today in capitalist countries the working class of the 19th century) remains the key to success.

International Communism and Russian National Policy

For thirty-six years at least from the Bolshevik seizure of power in Russia in 1917 to the death of Stalin in 1953, the

---

29. Such as Jack Woddis in *New Theories of Revolution*, Allen Lane/Penguin Press, 1972.

guidance if not the control of the revolutionary movement throughout the world was asserted by the Communist International (whatever its official title or anonymity), that is, the union of national Communist parties with the Communist Party of the Soviet Union as the dominant partner. Thereafter the operational unity of the Communist machine, outside the Soviet Union itself and the Eastern European countries under Russian military domination, was weakened chiefly for two reasons, both arising from its close link with the Soviet government. First there was the growing rivalry, both national and ideological, between Moscow and the China of Mao Tse-tung. Secondly there was the decision, dictated partly by the Chinese threat, partly by the desire to stabilize the nuclear stalemate with the United States, to cultivate a relaxation of tension with the Western powers. It is a common error, increased by much wishful thinking, to believe that because Soviet Russia for reasons of national policy has adopted for the time being this more astute course of action, which suggests no intention of territorial expansion (while steadily increasing its naval, land and air potential), the Communists are any less determined to promote world revolution than they always were. Peaceful coexistence, as Soviet leaders have constantly declared since Khrushchev made clear that the victory of socialism cannot come through nuclear war, means a continuance of the struggle by all means short of war. One of those means, certainly more effective than that of open threats to the national interests of the Western world—which among other things brought NATO into existence—is to court the general will for peace by such measures as the European Conference on Security and Cooperation, the proposals for balanced force reductions in Europe, and the flirtation with the United States. Much is made also of the opportunities provided by the multifarious resolutions of the United Nations by which, under the cover of peaceful intentions, active support is given to the vendetta of the Afro-Asian bloc against the "imperialists." The former tactic attracts the goodwill of governments and large sectors of public opinion. The latter, involving partisan support of the various "liberation" campaigns, terrorism included—from Indo-China, Africa and Palestine to Latin America—is less congenial to governments but appeals to the emotions of radical parties and religious groups in all the Western countries. It is by this means particularly that Catholics, as never before, are entangled in common pressure groups, demonstrations and subversive action in the promotion of Communist policies, and thus in the acceptance of the Communist ideology.

Totalitarianism in the Soviet Orbit

To diagnose the changing tactics of the Soviet government's diplomacy and their apparent effects is, however, to see only half the picture. It is not true, for instance, that the relative normality of life in the Soviet Union and Eastern Europe, compared with the Stalinist despotism, has altered the basic totalitarian character of the regime. Despite small courageous minorities of intellectual independents whose critical writings secure publicity in the West, the hold of the Communist *apparat* upon all aspects of life is as efficient as ever. Commenting upon the case of the scientist Dr. Zhores Medredev, who was forcibly detained in a lunatic asylum and eventually let out after much agitation and pressure both inside and outside of the USSR, Professor Leonard Schapiro writes:[30]

> In microcosm this case contains within it the quintessence of totalitarian rule; the superior power which can override all ostensible institutions; the subjugation of the legal order; the lack of discrete and separate organs of power—in short the omnipresence of *total* control over the individual.

This unchangeable, systematic oppression of the human spirit, which is manifested in the banishment of an increasing number of dissidents to rigorous labour camps in the Soviet Union today, is no less evident in the series of political trials in Czechoslovakia of those associated with the attempt of Dubcek to humanise socialism. Even in Romania, the most inde-

---

30. *Totalitarianism,* Key Concepts in Political Science series, Pall Mall Press, London, 1972.

pendent of the Eastern European states in its foreign policies, the rule of the Communist Party is as rigid as ever.

Communist Opportunism in Other Countries

Opportunism remains the characteristic of the central Marxist-Leninist power, whose greater or lesser direct influence upon Communist activities in other countries (e.g. Cuba, Chile, Guinea, India, Iraq) largely depends on the tactics of Russian foreign policy at any given time. The external revolutionary effects of Chinese policy are most evident only in certain selected parts of the world, (e.g. East Africa, Southern Arabia, Albania). It is, however, the general spirit or ideology of the Marxist-Leninist doctrine and system, more than any direction from Moscow or Peking, which moves the Communist parties in other countries to adopt whatever local tactic they consider best suited to advance the revolution. Thus the large French and Italian Communist Parties are using the electoral opportunities open to them. In France it is for this purpose that ecumenical cooperation with the Catholic Left has been so intensively pursued, especially since 1968. In England, where the Party is a small minority, efforts are concentrated upon securing key positions in student unions and in the large trade unions (e.g. engineers, dockers, automobile workers), whose inflationary wage demands can be pressed to the point of damaging strikes. In Spain, Portugal and Turkey, where the Party is outlawed, violent subversion is resorted to (e.g. the excesses of Basque nationalism; bombs in Lisbon docks; outrages against NATO personnel in Turkey). In such nations Communists also seek to infiltrate progressive minorities and to spread propaganda.

The "Liberation" Tactic

In Africa almost all the independent states are officially Socialist, though it is doubtful how far the theories of Marxism are understood except by a small number of the ruling intelligentsia. The chief practical advantage of socialism to the ambitious single-party leaders and to the military adventurers who

74

ultimately secure control, is as a formula for power, both against foreign industrial interests and against the ineradicable tribal traditions which are the chief obstacle to enforced uniformity. Emotionally, however, the revolution is most potent in the "liberation" movements directed against the Portuguese provinces, the South African Republic and Rhodesia, all of which movements, with one exception,[31] are now wholly Communist and mostly Chinese in organisation, operational control and equipment. The political importance of their intense propaganda, particularly in northern Europe and North America, far exceeds their relatively ineffectual military activities on the spot. Here, however, we find all the odious techniques of the revolutionary war which the *guerrilleros* have learnt from their Chinese, Soviet or Algerian instructors, such as the "selective terrorism" by which unarmed tribal chiefs and village headmen are systematically chosen for assassination in order to destroy the existing social structures. On a far greater scale and for nearly twelve years this inhuman terrorism has been practised by the Vietcong upon the unhappy villagers in South Vietnam; and it is not the least tragedy of the frustration of American intervention in that pitiless civil war that the emotional shock provoked throughout the world by the magnitude of the United States bombing operations quite obscured this most extensive and cruel Communist crime against humanity.

The "New Revolutions"

The "New Revolutions" are among the main political and military forms of the Marxist-Leninist revolutionary movement in various parts of the world. Many other forms are entangled with nationalist passions, as in Northern Ireland and the Arab world. What are we to think of the ragtag and bobtail of revolution which manifests itself in the rural guerrilla—which seems to have failed with Ché Guevara in Latin America, though not in the Philippines: the disjointed urban guer-

---

31. The UPA or FLNA, the Bacongo organisation whose headquarters are in Zaire.

rilla organizations, with their kidnapping and hijacking and the inevitable repression they provoke; the periodic disorganization of university and high school life, particularly in Western countries and Japan, by student revolutionaries; and the apparently senseless violence of young intellectual militants such as the Angry Brigade in England or the Baader-Meinhof gang in Germany? Most of these local collective resorts to violence cannot be attributed to international Communist direction; indeed, they are often an embarrassment to the considered strategy of the Communist Party. Yet there is a kind of osmosis of the spirit of rebellion, like a percolating fluid which links the local rebellions with one another and with the major manifestations of the World Revolution and, in the prevailing mood which Mr. Watt describes in the passage I have quoted, assures them of the warm sympathy of progressive opinion. In fact, if we analyse any or all of these revolutionary movements or organisations we find the essential characteristics I outlined on page 71. In particular there is the denial of any Divine source of authority; the belief in the right to use any means, however violent, to overthrow the existing order of society in the name of the class, race, nationality or party to which one has given one's allegiance; and complete disregard of the duty to respect the lives and rights of other human beings. What Marxist-Leninism has done, reinforced by its apparent military and political success over a great area of the Euro-Asian land mass, is to throw the mantle of an apparent world system over these basically anti-social and anti-moral elements, a system erected upon a supposed economic determinism and political inevitability, with the unattainable good of a classless society enjoying equality of material welfare as its justifying objective.

Conclusion

This is the Revolution as it exists in the world today. The author of *Théologie de la Révolution*, while denying that the endemic, continuous revolution for which he finds an inherent urge in Christianity is necessarily Marxist, admits that "throughout the whole world, any revolutionary movement meets Marxism on its way. We cannot speak of Christians in the Revolution without clearly stating the fact that, in the concrete, they will encounter Marxism on their way." There follows the passage quoted in the last chapter about the feasibility of cooperating in the revolutionary movement of the Marxist while leaving aside his atheism in the hope that it will fade away. It is, however, quite fatuous for Christian theologians to preach or encourage a revolution *in vacuo*. Not only has there never been a political revolution without the violation of human rights; but to pretend that the Marxist Revolution is not essentially atheistic in the face of the obvious and notorious evidence of two generations of atheistic education in Soviet Russia, in every one of the Eastern European countries under Communist rule—including Yugoslavia—as well as in China, is manifestly dishonest. What is entirely incompatible with the Christian religion is to pretend that in any political or economic system atheism, the denial of the existence of Almighty God, his love and his laws, *does not matter;* or that materialism, which is the repudiation of the universal moral law as well as the spiritual nature of man, *does not matter.* It is precisely this that *does* matter most in judging any human institution, however much opinions may legitimately differ about its economic merits or of the case for change in particular circumstances. It is this false sense of values which is the chief evil of the current idolatry of revolution.

Chapter 7

WHAT KIND OF CHRISTIANITY?

We have seen what, in the concrete, the Revolution means today. We must now examine the contention that the endorsement of the Revolution is inherent in Christianity itself.

There can be no doubt that the teaching and example of Jesus Christ and his apostles call now, as they have called these nineteen hundred years and more, for conversion and newness of heart. Consequently they inspire, under the guidance of the Holy Spirit who came to lead the Church "into all truth," a constant striving for the better by the Christian in every sphere of his life, spiritual and domestic, personal and social, stemming from his love of God and neighbour.

Nor can there be anything but sympathy for the passionate desire of Christians, such as those authors whose intemperance we have been obliged to criticize, who have seen at close quarters the crushing misery of the seemingly hopeless poor whether in parts of Latin America or Southern Asia or elsewhere, or the victims of racial oppression, to find means of remedying their afflictions.

But to leap from this honourable emotion to the conclusion that the whole message of Christianity must be turned and twisted to justify political revolution is to produce a sorry caricature of the one true religion. It involves such massive omissions of essential parts of the New Testament as to alter the whole balance of Our Lord's doctrine as shown in the Gospels and developed in the Acts of the Apostles and the Epistles. It ignores the overriding importance of the moral law and particularly of the Decalogue. Sin, grace, redemption and the rights and duties of the individual soul, as the proper recipient of the Divine Commandments, are either brushed aside or subordinated to supposed imperatives for collective action. The far from simple tasks of the Church in interpreting and applying throughout history the principles implied in Christ's teaching on civil authority, peace, the permissible use of force, social and international ethics and such matters, are disregarded, except in so far as the social doctrine of modern popes is either castigated or approved according to its opposition to or potential support for the revolutionary thesis. And nonsense is made of history.

The basic error of the revolutionary theologian's attempt to make a political or economic programme of the Gospel is surely that the whole teaching and appeal of Jesus Christ and his apostles were and are addressed to individual souls. Though much of this doctrine undoubtedly concerns the Christian's corporate participation in the unity of the Church and his social duties, it is yet for each, having free will, to respond or not to respond to the call. There is not one of the several "themes of Christianity" which the author of *Théologie de la Révolution* selects—repentance, conversion, hope, renovation, judgment and the rest—that is not quite evidently personal in its original application; nor is there any which can relate, without distortion, to collective action for political subversion.

The arbitrary selection of themes is itself enough to give quite a false picture of Christianity. Let us take first the most striking omissions. "The Devil can quote Scripture to his purpose"; and it would be equally misleading to interpret the social implications of the New Testament as enjoining solely obedience to civil authority, as it is to select the call to newness of life, repentance, the hope and promise of the kingdom of God and the liberty of the sons of God, and to build on these texts a case for habitual revolt against civil authority. Yet, while such special pleading on either side does not touch the basic purpose and consequences of the Incarnation and Redemption, it is true to say that the former is the subject of more explicit Scriptural injunctions than the latter. It is extraordinary that not one of the following lapidary texts is so much as mentioned in the "synthesis of Christianity" which the author of *Théologie de la Révolution* puts together.

Civil Authority

Take first the question of authority. The two most striking statements of Our Lord in this regard are, first, his answer when shown the coin of the tribute by the disciples of the Pharisees and Herodians, hoping to trap him: "Render to Caesar the things that are Caesar's and to God the things that are God's" (Matthew XXII, 15–22).

Secondly, the more far-reaching assertion of the Divine origin of all human authority contained in his answer to Pilate: "Pilate therefore saith to him . . . Knowest thou not that I have power to crucify thee and I have power to release thee? Jesus answered: Thou shouldst not have any power against me unless it were given thee from above" (John XIX, 6–16).

The positive duty to obey civil rulers is developed in most explicit terms by St. Peter and St. Paul in their Epistles. Their teaching has been quoted and developed time and again all through the Christian ages; indeed, there was a tendency in both the Calvinists and the upholders of the Divine Right of Kings in the 17th century to exaggerate it, without due regard to the right of subjects to disobey unjust rulers, which was elaborated, for instance, by the Neo-Scholastics in response to the important reservation of St. Peter, "We ought to obey God rather than men" (Acts V, 29). It must be remembered that the higher powers, to whom Christians were exhorted in the following passages to be obedient, were all authorities of a pagan empire. Nor is it only because all authority is from God, but because of the moral purpose of political authority, that they were so exhorted. St. Paul writes:

> "Let every soul be subject to higher powers. For there is no power but from God. Therefore he that resisteth the power resisteth the ordinance of God. And they that resist purchase to themselves damnation"—hardly an encouragement to the Christian to be a revolutionary. And the apostle concludes: "Where-

fore be subject of necessity; not only for wrath but also for conscience sake. For therefore also you pay tribute. For they are the ministers of God serving unto this purpose. Render therefore to all men their dues: tribute to whom tribute is due; custom to whom custom; fear to whom fear; honour to whom honour" (Romans XIII, 1–7).

St. Peter is not less forthright, and it is important to notice in the following passage that freedom, though not the abuse of it, is implied as consistent with subjection to lawful authority:

Be ye subject to every human creature for God's sake: whether it be to the king as excelling, or to governors as sent by him for the punishment of evil doers and for the praise of the good. For so is the will of God, that by doing well you may put to silence the ignorance of foolish men; as free and not making liberty a cloak for malice, but as the servants of God. Honour all men, love the brotherhood, fear God, honour the king (I Peter II, 13–17).

The Irrelevance of Servitude

More pertinent even to the claim that a principal theme of Christianity "coincides" with the call to revolution and liberation are the no less famous injunctions of SS. Peter and Paul to servants or, as the Greek is more properly translated, slaves. St. Peter continues in the same Epistle:

Servants be subject to your masters with all care, not only to the good but also the froward. For this is thankworthy: if for conscience towards God, a man endures sorrows, suffering wrongfully. For what glory is it if, committing sin and being buffeted for it you endure? But if doing well you suffer patiently, this is thankworthy before God (I Peter II, 18, 19)

St. Paul's injunctions are alike:

"Servants be obedient to your masters according to the flesh," he writes in his Epistle to the Ephesians (VI, 6, 5). This he repeats in his Epistle to the Colossians (III, 22), adding, "not serving to the eye, as pleasing men, but in simplicity of heart fearing God"; and again in his letter to Titus (II, 9, 10): "Exhort servants to be obedient to their masters, in all things pleasing, not gainsaying,

not defrauding, but in all things showing good fidelity that they
may adorn the doctrine of God our Saviour in all things."

And what is the hope to which they can look forward? Is it,
as the author of *Théologie de la Révolution* would have us
believe, one of the main themes of the New Testament, liberation from servitude to human masters? No; it is "Looking for
the blessed hope and coming of the glory of the great God and
our Saviour Jesus Christ" (Titus II, 13).

Are we then to believe that Peter and Paul positively approved the institution of servitude as an essential part of the
"social structure," to use the modern expression? Surely not.
Neither is there any sign of their condemning it, as they must
needs have done if the central theme of the Christian message
which they had to preach was political liberation. The aboli-
tion of slavery after many centuries; then the movement for
fair conditions of industrial labour; then the insistence upon
the dignity of the human person and the definition of essential
human rights upon which the popes of the 20th century have
laid such emphasis—all this may properly be seen as the slow
and logical evolution of natural justice interpreted by Christian charity, but constantly impeded by the sins of men, as it
always will be. But what these passages do show is that Christianity in origin and historically was *not* a political programme
at all. If the apostles took society as they found it, adjuring
slaves to obey their masters, masters to be benevolent to their
slaves, subjects to be loyal to their rulers; husbands and wives,
parents and children to fulfil their duties to one another, and
all, whatever their varied stations in life, to remember that
they were members one of another; it was because of something infinitely more sacred and compelling than any differences of function, class or social status or any political question.
It was the unity of the body of Christ in which all baptized
Christians are incorporated:

For as the body is one and hath many members, and all the
members of the body, whereas they are many, yet are one body:
so also is Christ. For in one Spirit were we all baptized into one

body, whether Jews or Gentiles, *whether bond or free* (I Corinthians XII, 12, 13; italics added).

The Organic Conception of Society

If there is one other thought which St. Paul develops in some detail in this magnificent chapter of his First Epistle to the Corinthians, it is the *inequality* of the different members forming the organic whole which the body is, some being more comely and more honourable than others. "But God hath set the members, every one of them, in the body as it has pleased him. . . . Yet much more those that seem to be the more feeble members of the body are more necessary. . . . And if one member suffers anything all the members suffer with it." Then, after distinguishing between the different orders and powers in the Church, which surely sets an ideal for the body politic very different from the jealous egalitarianism of today, he ends: "But be zealous for the better things; and I show unto you yet a more excellent way. If I speak with the tongues of men and of angels and have not charity I become a sounding brass or a tinkling cymbal . . ." Is not this central to the whole Christian ethos of society?

I have taken this question of slavery because it demonstrates in the most striking way the fact that the Christian revelation, whatever its gradual influence in the course of history upon the laws and customs of civil society, was not in any sense an economic or political programme. It is only by an extreme form of special pleading that the themes developed in Chapter 5 can be given that kind of political meaning. It is indeed true to claim that both the denunciations of injustice to the poor, widows and orphans by the prophets and Our Lord's blessing of those who "hunger and thirst after justice" must impel Christians to seek to remedy injustice, so far as they can, in any and every sphere of private and public life.

This is the impulse which made Blake's outburst against "the dark satanic mills" of the industrial revolution the theme song of the Christian Socialists in Britain; and not only of them but of so many thousands of English school children who have thrilled to Elgar's musical setting of the words of Blake's poem:

I shall not cease from mental fight,
Nor shall my sword sleep in my hand,
Till we have built Jerusalem
In England's green and pleasant land.

But the work of justice is the work of the head as well as the heart. For what determines justice in the life of society—domestic, industrial, national or international? It is the law of God; to which no attention, we find, is paid by the theologians of revolution. Yet unless we are clear what are the basic postulates of the natural law to which human government should conform, such minor questions as the conditions in which physical force may be used, either to maintain order or to vindicate civil injuries, cannot profitably be answered.

The New Commandment

There is of course a sense, far removed from the political, in which Christianity is revolutionary. Our Lord's new commandment of love and forgiveness of "those that trespass against us" gave a radically new set of values to life. Nicholas Berdyaev expressed this rhetorically when he wrote:

> The Christian is the eternal revolutionary who is not satisfied with any way of life, because he seeks the kingdom of God and his righteousness, because he aspires to a more radical transformation of man, of society and of the world.[32]

Yet this transformation is based intrinsically upon the *repudiation* of violence. In fact, if we were to select one theme of the teaching of Jesus Christ concerning the social order which distinguished it both from the Hebrew law and from the prevailing laws and customs of the Roman Empire, it would be far more the pacific, non-violent theme than any other. It was this that the earliest Christian Fathers taught and upheld in the face of persecution as their distinctive tenet, until the necessities of political responsibility within the Empire led to

---

32. "*La Afirmación Christiana de la Realidad Social,*" quoted in *Is Revolution Change?*

the inevitable development of the doctrine to allow for the restraint of disorder and the defence of society. It is in the fifth chapter of St. Matthew's Gospel that we find the fullest teaching by Our Lord of the spirit and principles upon which his followers are to base their whole activity in human society. To describe this, his Sermon on the Mount, as the "charter of liberty" is meaningless. Familiar as it is, we cannot fail to recall it.

Beginning with the beatitudes, he declares that the poor in spirit, the meek, the mourners, they that hunger and thirst after justice, the merciful, the clean of heart, the peacemakers and those who suffer persecution for the sake of justice are particularly blessed by God. He goes on to command his followers to be the light of the world. Then comes his confirmation of the Ten Commandments and in particular the Commandment "Thou shalt not kill," which he extends to include condemnation of the anger which may lead to murder. Then comes the injunction to seek reconciliation with brother or adversary; then the denunciation of every form of adultery and lust; then the prohibition of swearing. His sermon ends with the famous command to substitute love and forgiveness for violence and revenge:

> You have heard that it hath been said: An eye for an eye and a tooth for a tooth. But I say to you not to resist evil: but if one strike thee on thy right cheek, turn to him also thy left . . . You have heard that it hath been said: Thou shalt love thy neighbour and hate thy enemy. But I say to you love your enemies; do good to them that hate you, and pray for them that persecute and calumniate you; that you may be the children of your Father who is in heaven.

This is a hard saying. But who can deny that it is, in the moral order, the most distinctive and imperative theme of Christianity? Any "theology" which ignores or bypasses it is, by definition, false. However much the moralist may logically allow the natural right of self-defence, or the duty of protecting one's fellow men against injury—which are the bases of the permissible use of force in the cause of social justice (not excluding even the exceptional case of just rebellion)—it follows that these are all derogations from the Christian ideal. The rules of minimum force and of the last resort are in themselves an admission that patience, reconciliation, mutual forgiveness, forbearance, and abstention from violence, in short the overcoming of enmities by love, remain the norm of Christian society.

That in itself is a most powerful argument against the attempt to turn "Thy Kingdom come, thy will be done on earth as it is in heaven" into a call for constant civil war and revolution. No, it is, as the Preface in the Mass of Christ the King so admirably expresses it, to be "a kingdom of truth and life, a kingdom of holiness and grace, a kingdom of justice, love and peace."

Of the many other distortions of the Christian message recorded in Chapter 5 there remain two which particularly require refutation, one doctrinal, the other historical.

The Covenant

First the Covenant; for what the author has to say on this point represents in a confused way, I believe, a fairly widespread illusion of Christian or post-Christian addicts of Marxism, that they are a kind of Chosen People. "The people of the Covenant," he says, "means supplanting the reign of necessity by the reign of liberty, in the language of Marx, which is indeed the language of the Bible. . . . It is not blood, or land, or history, or geography, but a common creation which unites them. Their bond of association is their common pursuit of the future which God makes for them; that is their liberty." These are "the People of God made by the Covenant"[33] We have here a confusion of ideas between the Catholic Church and other baptised Christians, on the one hand, described by the Second Vatican Council[34] as "this messianic people" and "the new People of God succeeding to the chosen people of the Old

---

33. See page 56.

34. *Dogmatic Constitution on the Church,* Section 9.

Testament;" and on the other, humanity in general, which soon becomes "the people," which in turn becomes "the working class" led by the professional revolutionary party.

But the Covenant, Old and New, is nothing of the kind, as the Council makes clear. The Covenant is a particularly sacred bond or alliance between Almighty God and a people who accept his laws:

> God therefore chose the race of Israel as a people unto Himself. With it He set up a Covenant. Step by step He taught this people by manifesting in its history both Himself and the decrees of His will and by making it holy unto Himself. All these things, however, were done by way of preparation and as a figure of that new and perfect covenant which was to be ratified in Christ . . . Christ instituted this new covenant, that is to say the new testament in His blood (cf. I Cor. II, 25) by calling together a people made up of Jew and Gentile, making them one, not according to the flesh, but in the Spirit. This was to be the new People of God.

This is the Church. It is open to all men of all nations who believe in Jesus Christ and are baptised. But this people of the new Covenant is *not* the whole of humanity, still less can it be identified with a party claiming to revolutionize the world in the name of an economic or political theory which denies the very existence of Almighty God. It is, at the widest, those who are united by baptism, by faith in Christ and by charity. Among them is the true Catholic Church consisting of those who . . .

> "are fully incorporated into the society of the Church who, possessing the Spirit of Christ, accept her entire system and all the means of salvation given to her and through union with her visible structure are joined to Christ who rules her through the Supreme Pontiff and the bishops. This joining is effected by the bonds of professed faith, of the sacraments and of communion" (Section 14). "Taking part in the Eucharistic Sacrifice, which is the fount and apex of the whole Christian life, they offer the divine victim to God and offer themselves along with it" (Section 4).

"This is the chalice of my blood; the blood of the new and everlasting Covenant, which shall be shed for you and for many for the remission of sins." That is the focal point of God's People. It has nothing to do with such human combinations as mediaeval communes, or the Solemn League and Covenant of Scottish Puritans in the 17th century, or the *Contrat Social,* or the Communist International, or any political league or party, good, bad or indifferent.

Wishful History

Lastly let us look at the historical basis of the argument that, though Jesus Christ eschewed the nationalist and revolutionary aims of the Zealots and all use of force, and refused to become a temporal Messiah, the dynamic of his teaching and the character of his apostles were bound to act as a leaven of political revolution. "To throw men formed in the Old Testament world into the midst of pagan society is to cause fermentation, shock and revolution. At the least, it means planting in the heart of the Roman world a principle of permanent confrontation."[35]

But this in fact is just what did not happen. Following the apostolic example, the early Fathers of the Church[36] were, without known exception, emphatic in their loyalty to the imperial authority. Never did the Church support any revolt against the structure of the Roman Empire, even when the most abominable emperors like Nero reigned. On the contrary, having survived fierce persecutions, the Church permeated the system at every level, not excepting the legions; and, after the conversion of the Empire, sought through its rulers and its administration to use it to the best advantage. In very many cases it was the civil or military district of the Empire that became the Christian diocese. The great barbarian invasions found the popes normally on the side of the

---

35. See page 61.
36. E.g., St. Clement of Rome, St. Justin, Tertullian, Origen.

beleaguered imperial power, until the gradual conversion of the invading tribes and the reconversion of the Arians led to the creation of new churches in the north and west of Europe and on the Iberian peninsula. Even then the structure of the converted kingdoms and their hierarchies generally corresponded to the established Roman model. Roman law was preserved in the codes of many of these peoples, like the *Lex Romana Burgundiorum* or the *Lex Romana Visigothorum* of the early 6th century, and in its fullest form the *Corpus Juris* of the Emperor Justinian became the basis of the civil law of Europe. Canon law, developed in parallel but not in opposition to the civil law, completed the juridical framework of Christendom.

In the social sphere there was again no abrupt overthrow of Roman institutions. Rather, Christian influence steadily diminished the cruelties of the pagan legacy like the games, as the gladiatorial fights and the slaughter of animals in the Colosseum were called. Thus in Canons 9 and 11 of the Apostolic Constitutions, which represent what was believed in the middle of the 4th century to be the apostles' own doctrine, we find that baptism is to be refused to actors, gladiators and all who take part in the games.

As for the attitude of the popes to the emperors themselves, many as were the differences that developed, there was never any revolutionary attempt to overthrow the Byzantine emperors under whose rule the great general councils of Nicaea, Ephesus and Calcedon took place in the East. Indeed, the Constantinian Church has become an habitual object of reproach for the progressives. Though with the coronation of Charlemagne by Leo III in 800 A.D. the restoration of the Empire in the West introduced an era of many conflicts between the papacy and the emperors (of which Gregory VII's assertion of the superiority of the spiritual power against imperial pretension was the most epoch-making), it was itself remarkable evidence of the strong hold of the Roman imperial tradition. The Frankish king had put on the sandals and chlamys of a Roman patrician for his coronation in St. Peter's and was hailed as "Charles Augustus, crowned by God, the great and peace-giving Caesar."

90

Eventually the Empire ceased to be a political reality as a temporal form of the Christian people, being supplanted by national kingdoms. Reformation and Counter-Reformation added to the rivalries of sovereigns the bitterness of religious dissension. New responsibilities for the Church were opened up by the discoveries of other continents, and a new era of scepticism, the most serious enemy of the Christian conception of society, began with the rationalist Enlightenment and has continued in the godless sequel of our days. But if the notion of a supernational political society, which the Roman Empire was, has passed away, its memory, and more than a memory, remains in the form of the ineradicable tradition of the unity of European civilisation. It is this that, after so many internecine wars, inspires today the attempt to achieve political and economic unity in the European Community. More important, a spiritual empire wider than the Roman Empire ever was, embraces all the nations of the world; and it is from Rome that it is ruled by the successor of Peter, the Common Father, Servant of the Servants of God.

This, then, is the lasting legacy of that Roman Empire in which Christ was born and to which the apostles Peter and Paul enjoined their converts to be loyal. Viewing, even in this foreshortened way, the great sweep of history over nineteen centuries, it is surely impossible to deny the providential design which, instead of committing the Christian apostles and their followers to "permanent confrontation" in the Roman world, as our revolutionary propagandist pretends, encouraged them instead, as good citizens, to permeate and adapt to the glory of God the worldy *imperium* in which they found themselves.

If I have emphasised this Roman story, it is because the tendency to trace the continuity of a wished-for political ideology as something inevitable throughout the course of centuries, is a common feature of progressive fanaticism. It results in a complete travesty of history. Necessary as it is at all times to seek the reform of whatever is defective and inimical to the essential rights of persons and families in the organisation of temporal society, the overriding lesson of history is that civil peace and order are normally essential to enable the Church

91

to carry out her pastoral mission. For the same reason it can only frustrate that mission if the preaching of the Gospel is identified with political conspiracy and revolt, however arguable the demerits of the existing order. That, I believe, is what St. Paul would teach today as he did in his great Epistles in those early days of the Church.

And what, lastly, of the contention that the whole history of the Christian West has been a history of revolution? It is not a thesis that can be seriously maintained. The Gregorian reform of the 12th century was certainly of great significance in freeing the clergy from the bondage of feudal investiture, but it was in no proper sense of the word a revolution. There were indeed wars and uprisings aplenty, and heresies arising and suppressed throughout the Middle Ages, but no major transformation of society. The Reformation of the 16th century *was* a great spiritual rebellion, more radical than the schism between the Latin and Eastern churches. It destroyed the ecclesiastical unity of Western Europe and created political and psychological divisions that endure. But it is nonsense to pretend that there was before the end of the 18th century any revolution comparable *in kind* to the French Revolution, still less that this was in any sense the last in a sequence of revolutions which had characterised the Christian West. What made it *sui generis*, unprecedented, and the forebear of the Marxist-Leninist Revolution of the 20th century was that it gave expression for the first time to a complete repudiation of the Divine source of authority in human society. It is the attempt to derive all authority—and not merely the choice of those who wield authority—from the people instead of from their Creator which militates against the empire of the moral law, condemns the Church to conflict or uneasy compromise with the civil power, and has produced in the last half century the "democratic despotism" which de Tocqueville foresaw, the totalitarian state. That is the end to which the special pleading and the pseudo-history of the theologians of revolution would logically lead us.

Part Three

POLITICAL CAUSES
OF "REVOLUTIONARY
CHRISTIANITY"

Chapter **8**

THE EVOLUTION OF
COMMUNIST TACTICS 1953-1973

There are two ways of identifying the historical causes of the phenomenon we are studying, namely the contemporary effort to transform into a revolutionary agency the social doctrine and action of the Church. One is to observe from within the Church the development of the relevant theories and movements. The other is to discover and analyse the strategy of that secular organisation whose objective is the world revolution. The latter method we shall explore first; for the convolutions of Catholic prelates, theologians, spokesmen and writers in this field, interesting and important as they may be to members of the Church, are, when viewed from a detached standpoint, only one of many features of the contemporary scene which are of tactical value to the revolutionary cause. They are also more probably the consequences of the secular policies and activities by which that cause has been advanced in recent years than the product of Christian ideas.

It must be remembered that the exploitation of any existing popular movement or sentiment which may either have a divisive and therefore weakening effect within the capitalist countries, or create an atmosphere of opinion favourable to the current foreign policy of the Soviet Union, has always been a feature of Communist tactics. This is true to some extent also *mutatis mutandis* of the activities of Communist bodies inspired from Peking; but while both are motivated by variants of Marxism-Leninism and hostility to "imperialism," the Chinese variety is far less widespread and organically developed than the international Communist mechanism which takes its cue from Moscow. It follows, however, from the parasitic tactic of Communism (outside the Communist-controlled countries, of course) that many of the movements which they patronise and eventually penetrate may in themselves be perfectly legitimate from the ethical standpoint; the Resistance movements in occupied Europe during the Second World War are the classic example. The worldwide reprobation of apartheid in the South African Republic is another. Yet another is the revulsion against weapons of mass destruction. The moralist must always be on his guard, therefore, against indiscriminate condemnation of people sincerely engaged in national, social or economic causes in themselves worthy of support or morally indifferent, merely because they have been seized upon by the Communists for their own purposes.

We have traced in Chapter 6 the permanent addiction of the main Communist apparatus to the promotion of world revolution in alliance with the national policies of Soviet Russia by every means short of major war—which is the official definition of "peaceful coexistence." If we apply the motto *Respice finem* —Look at the end in view—what are the objectives which this power might hope to attain in the foreseeable future? They would seem to be:

(a) The weakening and eventual disruption of NATO.
(b) The neutralisation of Western Europe, both for the above purpose and to secure the Soviet rear in view of the Chinese threat.
(c) Maximum utilisation of anti-colonialist passion in order to complete the alienation of Africa from the West.
(d) Demoralisation of the social and economic structure of capitalist societies from within.

To which we might add detachment of Latin America from United States predominance and the extension of political influence to accompany the worldwide Soviet naval expansion, especially in the Indian Ocean and the Middle East.

If such were our purpose, what would we do to neutralise the traditional opposition of Christians and particularly of the Catholic Church and, if possible, win their support? We should, of course, play down the denial of God which is inherent in Marxist materialism and make the most of the Christians' desire for practical cooperation wherever possible. In this field we should find an immense advantage both in the rapid increase of secularism in the non-Communist world and in the new tendency of the Church to give priority to social causes. But in particular we should concentrate on three lines of approach: a) peace; b) anti-imperialism; and c) dissatisfaction with the values of capitalist society.

The object in every case would obviously be to channel Christian criticism of social evils and sympathy with the underdog—much of it genuine and justified—into the invariable Marxist formula of class war. We should expect belief in the inevitability of revolution to overthrow the structure of capitalist society to be encouraged, but with due regard to the existence or absence of "revolutionary situations" and with the use of "constitutional" methods wherever they are open either to Soviet diplomacy in the United Nations or to Communist parties in the parliamentary systems of democratic states. Meanwhile we should busy ourselves in the field of moral and political theory to undermine the traditional Christian opposition to violence, with the practical objective of recruiting the emotional support of Christian as well as socialist and liberal opinion for the bloody "wars of liberation" which are being waged under Communist direction in Southeast Asia and Africa as the sequel to decolonisation.

All this is exactly what has happened, particularly in the two decades since the death of Stalin. The acceptance of the practical consequences of nuclear stalemate with the United States has compelled Communist use of more patient and intelligent methods to promote, without the risk of major war, the twin but not always compatible objectives of world revolution and Russian foreign policy. In the process there has been a remarkable change in the technique both of senior Soviet propagandists and of Communist party leaders in their dealings with the Catholic Church, since they realize that the Church is one of the main elements of coherence in the European civilisation which they hope will disintegrate. A policy of dialogue has replaced both the abuse of religion as nothing but a weapon of the bourgeoise, and repetition of the Masonic anti-clerical clichés of the last century.

The diplomatic history of this phase is well known. The welcome given to Pope John XXIII's eulogy of the United Nations in his encyclical *Pacem in Terris*: the Pope's friendly reception of Khrushchev's son-in-law; the relative success of the Holy See's endeavour to improve the Church's condition in Eastern Europe; the fulsome Communist endorsement of Pope Paul's encyclical *Populorum Progressio;* the ecumenical exchanges of the Moscow Patriarchate with Rome. It is open to discussion which side has so far got the better of these manoeuvres, though it is undeniable that they have greatly encouraged Marxist penetration of the Catholic clergy, particularly in Western Europe and Latin America.

The Peace Campaign

What concerns us more is what has happened in the sphere of basic principles. Here it has been perceived by Soviet propagandists that the courting of the "peace movement" in the Western world, which has been the main means of weakening the morale of the capitalist countries for nearly forty years, cannot serve the purpose of enlisting the required support for the belligerent "liberation movements" and revolutionary operations in Latin America or subversive terrorism where it might come into play, as in Spain, Portugal or Turkey. Yet the appeal to pacific sentiment can always strike an answering chord in the West, from the papacy to the ordinary public, which, though it has lost the practice of religion, still retains a certain legacy of Christian attitudes. And the practical achievement of Communism, after all these years, is to have established throughout the political and religious Left of the non-Communist world—ignorant as it is of foreign realities—the fixed idea that Soviet Russia stands for peace, while it is the Americans and those whom they support who are the warmongers.

This operation started in the latter 1930's when the Western headquarters of the Comintern, having been driven out of Berlin, took refuge in Paris and, aided by the *Front Populaire*, set to work to mobilise the religious and political peace organisations—of which the British League of Nations Union was then the largest—"against war and fascism." The prime and understandable aim of this *Rassemblement universel pour la Paix,* as it was called, was to unite this body of peace-loving opinion in support of the Soviet Union, threatened, as indeed it was, by the military aggression of Nazi Germany. This new initiative won many allies among Western liberals and radicals for the Communist cause in the Spanish Civil War which broke out at that moment, and it is from the passionate climate of those days that dates—what had not existed before—the bond, as seen by those who dominate the press and mass media, between Communism on the one hand and social democracy and the non-conformist religious conscience of the Anglo-Saxon world on the other. Only a small minority of Catholics at that time, such as those in the English Labour Party, gravitated into that camp. Submerged during the embarrassing episode of the Molotov-Ribbentrop Pact, this strange alliance of opinion-makers blossomed again as soon as the Soviet Union, invaded by Hitler, became the ally of Britain and the United States. Indeed, there was no limit to the unqualified praise of the USSR handed out by the propaganda organs of United States Government agencies to women's organizations, colleges, etc. during World War II.

This, then, was the great volume of pro-Soviet opinion in the Western nations which was available to Moscow at that time. It was stupidly squandered by Stalin and henchmen like Zhdanov in their fury against President Truman and the Allies for thwarting, by their action in Greece and Germany, the Communist domination of Europe. Thus, when it came to using what remained of that asset for Stalin's new purpose, which was to oppose the growth of American nuclear power and the Atlantic Alliance, it was of very little use in the United States. Agitation against the Bomb was, however, soon a popular cause in Britain, France and the neutralist north in Europe. After the Stockholm Conference especially, the "Ban the Bomb" campaign launched a whole series of street demonstrations in London and other European capitals which were soon to become endemic for any cause patronised by Communism; and to this day thousands of ragged marchers, prams included, wend their weary way each Easter to Aldermaston, the English nuclear research centre, to protest against the bomb which is no longer made there. The whole of this emotional campaign, which had great influence upon the Catholic Pax Christi Movement, especially in France and Germany, was quite divorced from realities. It got under way when the United States was believed to have the nuclear monopoly, and when the progress of the Russians in developing nuclear missiles was secret: it never lost its essentially anti-American and anti-British character in denouncing the horrors of nuclear destruction and radiation. Here, as in many other popular causes, the repugnance to weapons of mass destruction which found its way into the acts of the Second Vatican Council with the favourite slogan of the movement, "a crime against God and Man," is a perfectly good motive. The achievement of Communist propaganda was to wed it to the spurious belief in the peaceful intentions of Soviet Russia.

Pacifism is still a well-worn line of Communist propaganda whenever it can be used to pin the responsibility for waging war upon the United States, as was done by a persistent distortion of facts in the case both of Korea and of Vietnam. It is also being refurbished now, in 1973, for that other central aim of contemporary Soviet foreign policy, mentioned above: to neutralise western Europe by the détente represented by the European Conference on Security and Cooperation, the negotiations on reciprocal arms reductions, and the advantage taken of Chancellor Brandt's *Ostpolitik*. But in so far as it represents a genuine hatred of armed conflict, pacifism has become rather an impediment than otherwise to the revolutionary cause in areas in which Communism is committed to prolonged violence.

The Right of Self-Defence Perverted

It is here that we see the more intelligent technique of official Communist propaganda now that exploitation of the "Leftward lurch" of the Catholic Church is seen to be of such importance to present Soviet strategy both in Europe and in the ex-colonial regions. Serious attention is now being given to some of the basic principles of social ethics which subsist in the Catholic tradition and which the old vocabulary of pacifist demagogy does not satisfy. Among those the most fundamental is the principle of self-defence against violence. This is a postulate of the natural law, instinctive in all men, which is recognized in Christian teaching as the one indispensable condition for the use of force in the last resort in the service of justice. Hence, in the works of Christian Marxists desiring to find justification for revolution and the subversion of the social structure, we find in the last few years the doctrine enunciated that whatever government, political or economic system the revolutionary desires to overthrow is itself a form of *injustice imposed by violence.* It is this that justifies or inevitably provokes violence as a form of self-defence by the subjects of that authority or the victims of that system. This oversimplification, which amounts to a distortion, of an important moral principle was very soon adopted by Communist propagandists and their instinctive followers.

This, as will be recalled from a quotation from Dom Helder Cámara on page 30, is the doctrine constantly enunciated by him and applied in the wildest way to the woes of the entire Third World (whatever that may be) oppressed by the injustice of "neo-colonialism," though the Archbishop himself, abstaining from the advocacy of violent revolution, deplores what he sees to be the fatal cycle. But the notion is accepted with no such qualms by the militants of the Left who have captured the Socialist parties, especially in Scandinavia, Britain and the Netherlands; the predominant American and British element in the World Council of Churches; many Catholic Justice and Peace Commissions in Western Europe; the Marxists who seem to have disoriented the French clergy and a sizable minority of the Spanish; and, of course, Catholic supporters of the guerrillas in Argentina and other South American countries. A wide diversity of other revolutionary groups, Trotskyite, Maoist and others among the students, echo the refrain. The political strike, as a step towards wrecking the existing system, assumed to be essentially unjust, is constantly engineered by trade union militants, notably in France, England and Italy. "The destruction of a society dominated by money and lying" is the objective of the Catholic Workers Action in France[37] and the class war is put forward as the necessary means to attain it. It is on the assumption of an essentially unjust capitalist system which does violence to human rights that both the militant Catholic progressives and a minority of the Protestant Federation of France, who secured control of its governing body, have since the "events of 1968" advocated violent revolution against this system as a Christian duty.

That was not the attitude of most of the Catholic hierarchy or of many of the more responsible French Catholic organisations to the student revolt of 1968. While sharing increasing sympathy with student demands for participation in a reformed university structure and for youthful repugnance to the constrictions of the consumer society, they called for Christians to be "the artisans of peace," for "constructive and fraternal dialogue" and the like, but opposed violence. It must be realised therefore that noisy as are the revolutionary organs such as *Témoignage Chrétien* and *Christianisme Social* and serious as is their influence, especially among urban priests, they are only a minority.

The most fantastic and ironical application of this pseudo-Christian doctrine of self-defence is that to be found in the attempted justification of "wars of liberation." It is of course perfectly arguable that the system of government in South Vietnam or Cambodia or Laos should be overthrown in favour of the Communist system of national socialism because that is the better system (if you believe it), or that the "detribalised socialism" which the FRELIMO or MPLA or PAIGC aim to establish in Mozambique or Angola or Portuguese Guinea is preferable to the obsolete "colonialism" of a European power which respects tribal traditions. But that alone would not bestir the righteous Christian indignation which is required. It has therefore to be made out that the Vietcong and the North Vietnamese army invading the southern parts of Indo-China, torturing and killing village headmen as part of their terrorist technique, were really *defending themselves* against unjust

---

37. To judge from its proposals to the Pastoral Session of the French Hierarchy at Lourdes in 1970.

aggression and tyranny. Even more farcically, it has to be pretended that the heavily armed terrorists invading Mozambique and Angola from Zambia and Tanzania, or their colleagues who bombard villages in Portuguese Guinea with Russian 122 mm rockets from a dozen miles away in Senegal, are really *defending themselves* against the Portuguese Africans whom they are murdering.

It is on this spurious basis that the financing of the unsuccessful "liberation" movements, all but one of which are wholly Communist in their direction, ideology and internal organisation, by the World Council of Churches is based, on the pretence of paying for imaginary humanitarian activities in areas which those guerrillas do not in fact control. It is typical of this unscrupulous propaganda that the Belgian Canon Houtart in his "sociological" study of *The Church and Revolution* (published in 1971, and not without merit on subjects with which the co-authors are personally acquainted) repeats the calumny about forced labour being prevalent in the Portuguese territories, despite the fact that this accusation was examined and completely disproved by a Commission of the International Labour Organisation in 1962.[38]

This is only the most flagrant example of the mess into which Christians are led by this ingenious attempt to justify violence on the general assumption that the existing political and economic system is itself the embodiment of violent injustice. Of course, even if we disregard the massive repression of liberties in the Soviet Empire, there may, as we have seen, be particular cases in which, as recognised by the Vatican Council, a government is guilty of prolonged and intolerable oppression and when, as a measure of desperation, revolt is inevitable. The southern Sudan, in which civil war is now happily ended, was, I believe, such a case. There is the difficult question of the South African Republic, in which without doubt there is the denial of essential natural rights to the black majority but where armed revolution would have no reasonable prospect of success and would cause great loss of life. In other parts of the

---

38. Endorsed by Mr. Pierre Juvigny's report to the ILO in January 1971.

world there are still cases—now rare—where industrial workers receive a wage insufficient for the minimum needs of family life; there are cases—far more numerous in Asia and Latin America—in which the system obtaining in the ownership and distribution of land leaves large peasant populations in a pitiful condition; there are appalling problems of urbanisation in developing countries. All these and many other social and economic defects cry out for urgent remedies, and remedies which by the nature of the case can only be provided by local authority within the framework of the nation concerned. But none of these excuse the removal of the restrictions which right reason and the Christian spirit impose upon a general recourse to violence.

Further, despite all the criticisms that can be levelled against financial monopolies and other defects of the capitalist world, one must remember the vast number of measures taken or under preparation at any given time in each of the Western countries to improve the standard of life and promote social welfare. In short, the truth is a very mixed picture of good, bad and indifferent and of widely varying situations in all parts of the world. For this reason alone the sweeping condemnation of a single economic system is bound to be false, and moral judgments based on that generalisation are bound to be worthless.

The Snare for Christians

The danger—and it is a real one for Catholics concerned with the social question—comes from identifying this Marxist generalisation (about the supposed violence inherent in the existing social order justifying an answering violence) with another kind of generalisation to which ecclesiastics are particularly prone. After describing in rhetorical terms the tribulations of the poorer parts of the world it is suggested, for instance, in the tendentious terms of the Roman Synod of 1971, that all this constitutes one great Injustice from which humanity must be liberated. So the aim of the revolutionary, instinctively followed by the progressive demagogue, lay or clerical, is to foist—quite unfairly—this new, generalised excuse for violence on to the remarkable impetus given by Pope

104

Paul VI from *Populorum Progressio* onwards, to the efforts of Christians in affluent countries to come to the aid of their needy brethren in the developing countries. For this purpose, quite regardless of the facts of history, the villain of the piece —against which the Communists would like to see the retributory violence directed—is singled out as the imperialist of yesteryear or the neo-colonialist of today. Many yards of anti-colonial resolutions, which the Afro-Asian delegations continue to pour out at the United Nations, serve to consolidate this false simplication of the world. It can only be a specific for war; but the most serious aspect of Christian entanglement in this sinister justification of violence is that it blinds people to the sin of murder as a means of attaining a doubtful political end. What cries to Heaven for vengeance is far less the imperfections of a polity or an economic system than the blood of hundreds of innocent people killed in Northern Ireland to promote the revolutionary nationalism of the IRA; of thousands of Indo-Chinese men, women and children slaughtered by the Communists—in the war which they initiated; of some hundreds of African tribesmen killed year by year in the anti-colonial cause by the terrorists financed by (among others) a group of Christian churches. Plausible nationalist or socialist arguments may be adduced for the ultimate objectives of each of these revolutionary undertakings, as well as for urban or rural guerrillas in other countries where there is social injustice; or the hijacking of aircraft; or the murder of diplomats by Palestinian fanatics to draw attention to the real grievances of their people against Israel. But it would be a fatal step for the Church ever to admit that what is intrinsically evil may be done in order that good may come. On this essential point the Pope is firm. Addressing the diplomatic corps accredited to the Holy See on the occasion of their New Year's visit to him in 1973 he said:

> Who will dare maintain that the ends justify the means, that terror may be an instrument of legitimate causes, that violent action against innocent people validly serves a cause that is deemed to be good?

Chapter 9

SEEDBEDS OF REVOLUTION WITHIN THE CHURCH

There are, of course, in all countries some Catholic personalities and groups who for personal or historic reasons have committed themselves to Marxist policies. There are, however, a few vigorous foci of militant socialism among the clergy which have been the most receptive to the recent Communist tactics described in the last chapter and the most active in their efforts to commit the Church to a revolutionary program. In Europe this tendency is more evident in the Latin part of the Continent than in the northern countries, where the main challenge to Christian orthodoxy comes from the sexual obsession. Similarly in the Americas it is in Latin America rather than North America that the revolutionary urge manifests itself.

France

The very active and well organized bodies of traditional Catholic laymen in France, such as those led by Pierre Debray and Jean Ousset, always declare that France is *"le centre même de la subversion"*—the very centre of the subversion of the Faith. Whatever the truth of this, it is certain that the majority of French Catholic periodicals such as the old daily *La Croix*, are now committed or friendly to the Marxist cause. The *Informations Catholiques Internationales,* whose influence is considerable throughout the world, can always be depended upon to diffuse articles and information inspired by the enthusiasms and hatreds of the Left as well as those reflecting modernist theology. *La Vie Catholique* and *Témoignage Chrétien,* both edited by Dominicans, are unreservedly Communist and revolutionary, and a number of smaller religious periodicals hardly less so. How great an influence for these views in the French Church can one deduce? There is evidence that 70% of the priests in the country are thoroughly disorientated and discredited with their people, but it is probably more the desacralisation of the liturgy and their pathetic attempts to be imitation laymen that has been the undoing of many than commitment to social revolution. There is, however, a substantial minority caught up in the current Marxist hysteria, who like minorities of Catholic progressives in other countries lobby and pressure the bishops, being particularly active in the pastoral councils, conferences and commissions with which the Church is now lumbered, in such a way as to give the impression that they represent the majority of the faithful. Almost certainly they do not; but the result at the episcopal level is the familiar reaction: either the episcopate says nothing on the social question or its utterances are so sibylline as to avoid any offence to the progressives.

Of about 32,000 priests, secular and religious, in France some 800 are known to have joined the extreme organisation *Echange et Dialogue,* which is wholly committed to the class war; a number of them are active without episcopal permission in trade unions or have broken their vows of celibacy. That is not a very high proportion of the whole; but one can judge from the tone of such erstwhile orthodox associations as the Young Catholic Workers (JOC) and the *Action Catholique Ouvrière,* now aggressive spokesmen for the class war, how widely Marxism has penetrated the clergy and other leaders involved with industrial workers. A great deal of the wastage in the seminaries and novitiates is attributed to the infection of those preparing for the priesthood by the Communist ideas which they pick up from the students of secular universities and high schools with whom they mix freely. At any rate the general tendency to degrade the distinctive character of the priest and to emphasise his supposedly social as distinct from his sacred function, is certainly killing vocations. Mgr. Frételière, in a working paper presented to the Conference of French Bishops at Lourdes in October 1972,[39] suggests that the best solution is to close the seminaries and to institute "information circles where young men who have a mind to consecrate themselves to the priesthood will live immersed in the environment of real life, in the workers' world for some, in the university for others." "It is hardly surprising," as Henri Fesquet wrote in *Le Monde* (29 October 1972), "that the seminaries are emptying when nobody, or almost nobody, is able to say what exactly a priest is, or what he is for."

The immediate, particular objective of the French Communist party during the last year has probably been to swell Catholic support for the newly formed *Front populaire*, the coalition of Socialist and Communist parties which hoped for a majority in the parliamentary elections of March 1973. They certainly succeeded in increasing their vote. The sly way in which Catholic opinion is courted is well illustrated by the following interview with Georges Marchais, now Secretary General of the French Communist Party, published by *La Croix* (19 November 1970),[40] of which hundreds of thousands of copies were distributed at church doors after Mass.

> The construction of the socialist society does not require the acceptance of materialism by all citizens. It means something quite different: the transfer to the nation of the ownership of the major means of production and exchange and the exercise of power by the workers, by the mass of the people. Is there anything opposed to that in the Christian faith? I do not believe there is.

French influence in the intellectual life of Europe, including Rome and the Francophone world, is considerable, which is why the commitment of the French Church to the revolutionary cause would be an important victory for international Communism. That influence is felt in neighbouring Belgium and Switzerland particularly; Louvain—or rather the French-

---

39. Reported in *Courier Hebdomadaire de Pierre Debray*, 2 November 1972.
40. Quoted by Marcel Clément in *Le Christ et la Révolution*, Paris, 1972.

speaking half of that Catholic university—is the happy hunting ground of Marxist theologians. The Swiss university of Fribourg, controlled by the Dominicans, is now notorious for its modernist ethics.

One has to look far into the past for reasons why the French Church has been so gripped by the anti-capitalist propaganda of Marxism-Leninism, especially since the Council. The powerful reaction against imperialism resulting from defeat in Indo-China and the traumatic effects of the Algerian war must be taken into account. Basically, however, the fact is that the Church suffers from a false guilt complex arising from the perpetual accusation of the anti-clerical Left that it is the religion of the Ancien Régime or at least of the bourgeoisie. The accusation is obsolete and, on the whole, untrue, since most of the priests since the complete separation of Church and State have in fact been poor and hardworking with no social pretensions. But it is true that, despite all the efforts at Catholic workers' circles in the latter 19th century and other well-intentioned schemes to promote the workers' welfare in a Christian setting, atheistic socialism secured a firm grip upon the urban proletariat, who were thus largely alienated from the Church. Consequently, effort after effort was made by the bishops to regain the industrial working class for Christianity, of which the experiment of the worker priests was one. It ended, as could have been foreseen, by many of these devoted men identifying themselves with the Marxist policies of their labouring friends' trade unions. In the process the tendency of the Church has been to fall over backward to prove itself the friend of the working class and not of the well-to-do. It was a fatal posture which, just as it led to the virtual loss of the Christian Trade Unions' identity in the Marxist mass, also exposed an ill-defended priesthood to the full force of Communist propaganda in its new and subtler forms.

Spain

The reasons for the rapid extension of economic and political modernism and Marxism among the Spanish clergy are different. It is part of the revolt against the authoritarian regime of

General Franco which, while it seems to enjoy the confidence of the majority owing to the prosperity and freedom from civil strife which it has brought to Spain, finds itself increasingly challenged on the labour front and in the universities. The demand for greater liberty is, of course, stimulated and exploited by the suppressed Communist Party; and the militant Basque nationalist organisation, ETA, is entirely Communist. The measures taken to suppress this defiance of the government's authority are much publicised to excite pity and protest in the foreign press and television. The international agitation on behalf of the eight ETA defendants convicted of murder in 1971 was a striking example of this tactic.

All this excites the sympathy of a certain number of the Spanish clergy, the more so as the liberal spirit of the Vatican Council is in conflict with the traditional attachment of the Church to the civil power and has led the Holy See to assert its independence by the appointment to vacant sees of new bishops, very different from those whom the government would have chosen.

This atmosphere is particularly favourable to the prevalence among the clergy of that Marxist infiltration of "social Catholicism" which, with its clichés of "liberation," we have seen to be so effective in France. Again, it is difficult to judge exactly what proportion of the episcopate and priesthood is affected. As one might expect, it is chiefly through the capture of a commission or an embryonic pastoral council that collective expression is given to the new religion; but, as we shall see by the treatment accorded by the Holy See to the Theses approved by a so-called General Assembly of Spanish Bishops and Priests held in September 1971, the Sacred Congregation of the Clergy had good reason to doubt its claim to represent the clergy of the country. The new Archbishop of Madrid, Cardinal Henrique y Tarancon, seems to lead the van, if we are to judge by his insistence at the Roman Synod that such social "facts" as colonialism and cultural or economic domination and oppression are sins in the Gospel sense.

It was the Justice and Peace Commission of the Spanish Hierarchy which denounced the "state of affairs provoked and maintained by the materialistic capitalist system which dominates our society"; but the fuller effusion of the General Assembly made it clear that this is only to be replaced, in the view of its adherents, by a new Marxist materialism. The following are extracts from the Document of the Sacred Congregation for the Clergy in reply to the Conclusions and Theses adopted by that Assembly. They provide a synthesis of the errors which go to make up in all parts of the world the caricature of Christianity adjusted to Marxism which the Theologians of Revolution find it so agreeable to contemplate:

Overall Analysis

1) "An equality is postulated between 'the faith of Mother Church and the ideology of the modern world' when it is affirmed that one must achieve a synthesis of the two, omitting what is unserviceable and taking what is good, in one as in another." But it is "the demands of the modern world upon the Church" which are understood . . . as the divine test of the authenticity of the Christian faith, "and this world is understood as being a determined *Weltanschauung* having a universal, irreversible, necessary and wholly positive character."

2) "The accentuated democratic conception of the Church" is next criticised as being practically identical to the one which appeared at the Synod of Pistoia in 1794 and was condemned. This involves "a genuine leveling of all believers—bishops, priests, laymen"—at least a functional levelling—by means of ambiguous references to "the one mission of the Church," to "collegiality," to "coresponsibility and so forth. . . . And so, while a civil job is demanded for priests, a participation in political life, etc., laymen are asked to be inserted in all ecclesiastical structures, to preach sermons, to administer the Eucharist, etc."

3) "There is a continual tendency to dissolve the action of the Church into a socio-political action which conditions the 'other' pastoral activities. . . . The commitment of the sacred ministry and of the Church as such to this politico-economic liberation is postulated as essential, admitting in some cases of partisan political activity by priests, activity which can take on from time to time a violent character. The primacy which is constantly attributed to this 'liberation' brings with it a collectivist conception of morality and of salvation: the 'supreme good' is an ambiguous social 'communion.' Sin is often reduced to the injustices (real or presumed) of the politico-social order."

Detailed Analysis of the Chapter

Among many detailed criticisms, the following are particularly relevant to the subject of this book; first, the twisting of papal encyclicals and documents of the Council to sustain the revolutionary thesis (cf. Chapter 5); second, the essentially materialist character of the new dispensation, which is to replace the injustices of the existing structure of society.

> There is an attempt to create a foundation for these ideas in the Magisterium of the Church. . . . This is done by putting together a sort of mosaic of texts from the Constitution *Gaudium et Spes* (On the Church in the Modern World), from the Encyclicals *Pacem in Terris* and *Populorum progressio* and from the letter *Octogesima Adveniens;* these texts, put one after another, outside of their proper context—from which they receive their sense and bearing—constitute a particular political program, in whose favour are adduced the well-known Gospel texts which have been abused for this purpose for some years.
>
> A strong basic argument is taken from sociology, by means of statistics, investigations, etc. (almost all taken from the same source whose inspiration is obvious) which are heaped up for purposes of prophetic denunciation of injustices, faults, defects, etc. of the strictly economic order. . . . On the one hand, there is nothing but talk of economic questions, of material means, of consumer goods (and not precisely basic necessities: automobiles, televisions, washing machines, refrigerators, etc.) and, on the other hand, the Spanish people are accused of materialism, of having no other aims beside material well-being. One gets the impression that what is being lamented is a certain diffusion of the capitalist mentality (this materialism is mentioned explicitly) by taking sides with a socialist materialism (which the text wants to present as a noble aspiration for justice which must be accommodated). The indubitable defects of capitalism are considered the ultimate sin, the origin of almost all social and personal evils, while there is not a word of reprobation for Marxism, atheism, etc.

And a little later on:

> It is also said that the Church needs to be "separated from every territorial power, in order to animate and participate in the historic movement of human liberation." This turns into a con-

tradiction unless by "territorial power" one intends to signify the civil authority and all other non-Marxist social forces, and by "historic movements of liberation," the Communist States, Marxist-inspired subversive movements, etc.—examples could be multiplied from the chapter and its attendant documentation.

The Spanish report is returned with these and many other criticisms with the request that at the next plenary meeting of the Spanish Episcopal Conference "everyone prescind from Chapter I and its propositions, which seem to be unacceptable both doctrinally and pastorally; and that Chapter II be replaced by the document on the ministerial priesthood approved by the last Synod of Bishops."

The document was signed in Rome on 9 February 1972 by John Cardinal Wright, Prefect of the Congregation, and by Archbishop Pallazini, Secretary. It is of capital importance as an authoritative demonstration of the incompatibility with the Catholic religion of the attempt to combine Christianity with revolutionary Communism. The Archbishop of Madrid did not like it. In its final considerations, the Congregation showed that it was not deceived by the pretensions of the General Assembly, which are typical of the claims made by progressive intriguers for any of the new quasi-official democratic bodies of the "post-Conciliar Church" which they are able to penetrate and control. It noted the burning polemics which the Assembly's proposals had aroused among the faithful in Spain, the concrete and verified evidence which it had received that they did not represent the views of the Spanish clergy as a whole, the gerrymandering employed in the recruitment of the Assembly, and the irregularities in its procedure. It was a welcome exposure.

Latin America

While these developments in France and Spain, which of course have their echo on a smaller scale in other European countries, show the formulation and expression of the distinctive theories of the new caricature of Christianity which the Marxist distortion of its social mission involves, it is from Latin America that comes the real drive for committing the Church to the Revolution. Very different as are the economies, populations and resources of the Latin American republics—from the almost entirely European and relatively prosperous lands of Argentina and Uruguay to the mainly Indian and impoverished population of Bolivia, from the great expanding economies of Brazil and Mexico to the small Central American and Andean republics with their persistent relics of landed oligarchy, poverty and political instability—their peoples are all Catholic. This in itself, with the increase in communications, the common dependence of their governments upon and the popular reaction against the financial and political preponderance of the United States and the much publicised tendency of the United Nations agencies to generalise the economic and demographic problems of Latin America as a single whole, gives the Catholic body—hierarchy, priests, intellectuals and demagogues—of these countries a greater impulse towards common thought and action than existed before. Among the elements which thus tend most quickly to communicate and unite, despite the very real national differences and rivalries of the continent, are those inspired by the propaganda of the world revolution. Others, rightly disturbed at social evils in their own countries, are attracted by the hope of radical change without any clear idea of how to bring it about. To all of these the success of the Cuban Revolution in 1959 made a powerful appeal. From this date the various eruptions of violence: first of the rural guerrillas, notably in Venezuela, Guatemala, Bolivia and Colombia, which yielded the young heroes Ché Guevara, Regis Debray and the priest Camilo Torres to the martyrology of the Left; then, when the complete failure to arouse the peasantry had shown the Castro model to be of no avail, the more sophisticated urban guerrilla with his killings and kidnapping, chiefly in Uruguay, Brazil and Argentina.

While there is little doubt that the bulk of the articulate public in all these countries has been and is on the side of the forces of order who have, with few exceptions, defeated or repressed the guerrillas and their suspected accomplices (not without the drastic police methods of which so much is made by their foreign supporters), there can be no doubt of the deplorable poverty of large numbers of people. There are the Amerindian peasantry in Bolivia and other Andean and Central American republics existing at a bare subsistence level; the inhabitants of the miserable shanty towns surrounding every big city; the crowded and underemployed population, largely of Negro origin, in the northeast of Brazil, to mention but a few examples. The egotism of a minority who own the greater part of the land in many of these countries, despite partial agrarian reforms, is also notorious. No bishop or priest who, knowing these evils, did not want to remedy them would be worth his salt. The debate about how to do it is therefore perfectly genuine and healthy. It is the argument to yield, or not to yield, to the desperation of violence which divides the Catholic community in every Latin American country.

The fact that the advocates of violence are everywhere in the minority is compensated by the fact that they have the progressive orchestra of the outer world with them and most of all, of course, the centres and publications of revolutionary Catholicism in North America and Western Europe. The human links between the two include the foreign missionaries and priests, Protestant and Catholic, who have gone to work in Latin America. Many of these become identified with the rebels and share their fate, being expelled or forced to return home. The Maryknoll missionaries expelled from Guatemala and elsewhere have no kindly feeling for the authorities, just as the Baptists have never forgiven the repression after the Angolan outbreak of terrorism which their protege organized. Camilo Torres, the brilliant young priest who eventually asked for laicisation in Colombia to join the guerrillas and was killed in 1966, had been Vice Rector at the Latin American College at Louvain. From Louvain too come the authors of two of the principal books on revolution which we have noticed, the Abbé Comblin and Canon Houtart. The latter's *The Church and Revolution*[41] is published by Maryknoll, whose own publication *Between Honesty and Hope: Documents from and about*

---

41. *The Church and Revolution* by François Houtart and André Rousseau, Orbis Books, Maryknoll, New York, 1971.

the Church in Latin America, is the source of much of his section on Latin America. (Maryknoll is the popular name of the Catholic Foreign Mission Society of the United States—the official organization of the Catholic hierarchy.) There are, therefore, apart from the general press and mass media, important centres both in the United States and Europe for the diffusion of all that concerns progressive and anti-authoritarian developments in the Catholic Church in Latin America.

It is characteristic of such books that, while the difficulties and controversies of the Church's social action are ostensibly described "sociologically," attention being given to all schools of thought, it is the revolutionary which always emerges as the "real thing," the criterion by which all others are judged. Thus Canon Houtart criticises Pope Paul VI for rejecting violent revolution as a means of creating a new society in his speeches at the Medellin Conference of Latin American Bishops in 1968:

> Should not the repressive nature of the power structure be the target of his condemnation rather than the revolution? And on a deeper level, when the Pope seems to advocate gradual change as an alternative to revolution, his proposition seems to rest on a very questionable foundation, for any such gradual change means a long-term work of educating the masses.

And a little later on with reference to "a critique of the institutional Church and the way it exists and functions in Latin America today," he writes:

> If a Christian can and must be a revolutionary in the face of present conditions, and if the duty of a revolutionary is to make revolution, what are the specific options he is faced with? This is a question which faces laymen and priests alike and the object of so much discussion and conflict. More and more Christians, both lay and clergy, seem already to take for granted that they must commit themselves to the revolution.

"More and more?" Even allowing for Mr. Allende's Socialist and Communist supporters in Chile, the minority political parties, where they exist, as in Argentina and Venezuela and the little groups of guerrillas throughout the continent, one wonders whether it would not be an exaggeration to say that 10% of the Latin American population is in fact revolutionary.

Though Camilo Torres is criticized in this work for his impetuosity, there is no doubt that he is the hero of the whole story:

> As he put it, "I am a revolutionary as a Colombian, as a sociologist, and as a priest. . . . As a Colombian I cannot be a stranger to my people's struggles. . . . As a sociologist, thanks to the knowledge I have of reality, I have arrived at the realization that technical and effective solutions will never be obtained without a revolution."

Such is the temper of a very typical account of the contribution made by the Church in Latin America to the revolutionary cause. It is evident that there is much diligent organisation of the revolutionary potential among the priesthood. Among examples quoted by Canon Houtart are a letter signed by 300 Brazilian priests in August 1967; another signed by 80 Bolivian priests criticizing some bishops for leading a demonstration against the guerrillas; another signed by 900 Latin American priests entitled "Latin America: Continent of Violence" and addressed to the Medellin Conference. It is not possible to verify these statistics. But we may take it that groups like the "Priests of the Third World" in Argentina and Brazil represent a substantial minority of the younger clergy of the continent.

Part Four

THE CHRISTIAN SOCIAL ORDER

Chapter 10

ESSENTIAL PRINCIPLES

What is depressing about the cult of revolution is its negative character. It is more concerned with destruction than construction. Its slogans are denunciatory and abusive and, though some of the economic and political situations which are the objects of its attacks undoubtedly call for urgent remedy, no clear picture emerges of the ideal society which it is hoped to construct, beyond variants of the general thesis of public ownership of the means of production in place of the evils which it denounces. The individual is sacrificed to the collective; and it is the professional revolutionary who determines the collective will. Communism is a formula for power. This appears in its ugliest form in the tactics of revolutionary war.

The Christian ground plan of the good society, to which such a wealth of teaching has been devoted by popes from Leo XIII to Paul VI, is, on the other hand, essentially *personal*. It is positive; it aims to serve the real needs, spiritual as well as material, of various sorts and conditions of men and their families. Though papal social doctrine certainly suffered from a late start compared with the grip which socialism had secured upon the industrial workers of Europe in the latter part of the 19th century, the Church has in compensation the benefit of many lessons learnt from the practical experience of Western countries, especially during the ascendancy of Christian democracy which synchronized with the period of European economic recovery after World War II, as well as the lessons learnt from an unprecedented missionary expansion.

The Natural Law

It is not, however, in the theories of economic and political organisation applied to the changing requirements of the modern world, valuable as they are, that the chief merit of Catholic teaching lies. It is in its insistence upon certain basic principles of the natural law which any form of human society must respect.

We may pause here to observe that any rejection of this law, by which Almighty God governs his creatures, and especially any denial of the objectivity of the moral law which determines their mutual rights and duties as well as their duty of obedience to God himself, is wholly incompatible with the Church's social mission. The Marxist-Leninist denial of God and of any moral standard other than the interests of "the masses" interpreted by "the Party," makes any union of Christian and Marxist social planning fundamentally illogical and dishonest, however the would-be political ecumenist may delude himself; though there are of course many activities of a practical nature to which a Communist state is constrained by the natural law which it cannot escape and in which its subjects rightly take part. In the same spirit the Holy See necessarily has to treat with Communist as well as with other established governments with a view to securing tolerable conditions for the hierarchy and the faithful within their territories.

Equally hostile to the Christian social order are "situation ethics," and the "existential ethics" invented by some modern, chiefly German, theologians, according to which "the general moral norms do not cover the existential moment of self commitment in a concrete situation, and therefore cannot tell the individual what he must do. In other words the will of God for an existing individual in a concrete situation cannot be adequately expressed in terms of conclusions from the natural law."[42] This notion inevitably degenerates into subjectivism. Obviously, circumstances affect the detailed application of the moral law. But once its objectivity and universal empire are

---

42. *The New Catholic Encyclopaedia.*

denied, what happens to such bedrock Commandments as *Thou shalt not kill, Thou shalt not steal, Thou shalt not commit adultery, Thou shalt not bear false witness?* These are fundamental to rationally and morally organized society. This is of great relevance to our subject; because any theory which erodes the objective moral obligation to abstain from personal or collective violence or breach of faith undermines the psychological foundation of peaceful order.

The Person

What then are the basic principles? The first is that politics are made for man, not man for politics; and by man is meant not the human race in general but individual men, women and children, especially as they are united in families. The first section of the long Pastoral Constitution of the Second Vatican Council, *Gaudium et Spes,* is entirely devoted to the dignity of the human person, expounding the teaching emphasised by John XXIII in his encyclical *Mater et Magistra:*[43]

> The social doctrine of the Catholic Church hinges on the principle that, necessarily, the foundation, cause and purpose of all social institutions are individual human beings; men, that is, who are social by nature and are raised to an order of things which surpasses and subdues nature.

And what is the distinctive characteristic of these persons whom all social, economic and political institutions exist to serve? It is that they are made in the image of God, having immortal souls and intellects. They are never merely consumers or producers of material goods, still less a *Lumpenproletariat* to be pushed around in the mass and exploited for political ends. When the Council comes to consider the economic needs and status of men, it says:

> In the socio-economic realm, too, the dignity and total vocation of the human person must be honoured and advanced along with

---

43. 218, 219.

the welfare of society as a whole. For man is the source, the centre and the purpose of all socio-economic life.

It is not therefore the political and economic laws and operations of socialist, capitalist or other states at any given time which are necessarily in conflict with the Christian social ideal, though some certainly are. What is inadmissible is any system which denies the spiritual nature of man and the essential rights and liberties which flow from it. That is why the materialism and *impersonalism* of Marxism-Leninism, like any form of totalitarianism which enslaves the individual to the absolute claims of class, race, nation or state, is wholly incompatible with Christianity.

It follows that all human institutions must ultimately be judged by the service which they render to the person; this applies to state and nation, to the choice and change of governments. All are of relative, none of absolute value. This is the direct antithesis of the idolatry of politics which is perhaps the most malign contribution Marxism has made to the social concepts and habits of the modern world. The Christian aim is always to harmonise the rights of man as an individual but social being with his duties to the societies of which he forms a part: domestic, religious, industrial, civic, cultural, professional and political.

The Family

Of human societies, the most important in Christian teaching is the family in which, from the moment of conception in his mother's womb, first the vegetative and animal life, then the intelligent life of the child unfolds. Here the human being, having the same nature as all his fellow men whatever their race or colour, receives the differentiation which comes of inherited customs, language and tradition. "Humanity," wrote Thomas Mann,[44] "oscillates between the law of differentation and the law of integration"; and, though he was writing of the necessary synthesis to be achieved between the requirements

---

44. *L'Esprit International* 1927.

of different nationalities and the common good of the international community, the same is true of the need of harmonising the distinctive life of the family and the group of families united by tribal or national traditions with that of the larger political society in which history has placed them and which they need for their security and development. Apart from the respect due to the family as a divinely created society which precedes the state, two attributes of the family are particularly emphasised in Catholic teaching. One is the right to own property, the other the right to educate.

Private Property

While the emphasis in papal teaching has varied from Leo XIII to Paul VI between the natural right to private property in itself (which has always been maintained) and the duty to share worldly goods with one's fellows who are in need, since God created the earth for the benefit of all, the importance of property to the family has been consistently stressed. Thus John XXIII, quoting in *Mater et Magistra* a broadcast of Pius XII's:[45]

> It is the function of private property to assure to the father of a family the real liberty he needs to enable him to discharge the duties laid upon him by the Creator concerning the physical, spiritual and religious well-being of his dependents.

It follows that the widest distribution of property and especially land among families is a favourite theme of papal teaching, just as the abuses resulting from the excessive concentration of wealth are vehemently denounced. It is denied that collective ownership by the State may ever replace private ownership, though in the course of time the popes, from Pius XI onward, have recognised the necessity of the State's ownership of public services and its control of certain vital industries, particularly when they are owned by too powerful financial groups to the detriment of the citizenry. The object in all such

---

45. *La solennita della Pentecoste*, 1 June 1961.

cases is, not to destroy, but to protect the natural right of persons and the family. It is the same distrust of the Leviathan of the over-powerful state which causes the popes to teach the important *principle of subsidiarity.* It was defined as follows by Pius XI in his encyclical *Quadragesimo Anno:*

> Just as it is wrong to withdraw from the individual and commit to a group what private enterprise and industry can accomplish, so too it is an injustice, a grave evil and a disturbance of right order, for a larger and higher association to arrogate to itself functions which can be performed efficiently by smaller and lower societies. This is a fundamental principle of social philosophy unshaken and unchangeable. Of its very nature the true aim of all social activity should be to help members of the social body, but never to destroy or absorb them.

Education

More immediate, because it has become the central battleground between the defenders of the Christian tradition of faith and morals and the sex-ridden modernists who, since the Second Vatican Council, have conspired within the Church to destroy that tradition, is the question of the education of children. The right and duty of parents to educate their children have always been taught by the Magisterium of the Church, but it was in the latter part of the 19th century that the pretensions of Liberals and Socialists stirred the popes to the vigorous defence of parental rights. Since then a vast proportion of the schools of Europe and North America have passed into the hands of secular authorities. Yet in Eastern Europe, under atheist rule, it is an astonishing tribute to the fidelity of millions of Christian parents—in Hungary for nearly thirty years, in Yugoslavia for most of that period, in Czechoslovakia and Eastern Germany—large, practising Catholic communities survive today, despite the almost total impossibility of teaching religion anywhere but in the home. In Poland fortunately the strength of the Church was too great for the Communist authorities to prevent a certain amount of religious teaching. The irony of the present situation is that it is in the United States, which vaunts its political freedom, that we find the most insidious attack on parental rights through the highhanded action of ecclesiastical bureaucracies, which in many parts of the country control religious education. Yet Leo XIII wrote:[46]

> They who would break away from Christian discipline are working to corrupt family life and to destroy it utterly, root and branch. . . . It is then incumbent upon parents to strain every nerve to ward off such an outrage, and to strive manfully to have and to hold exclusive authority to direct the education of their offspring, as is fitting in a Christian manner; and first and foremost to keep them away from schools where there is a risk of their drinking in the poison of impiety.

Whereas papal teaching on this subject had been specifically concerned to safeguard Catholic education and the rights of parents in regard to it, the Second Vatican Council, basing itself on the requirements of the natural law in its Declaration on Religious Freedom, asserted the right of all religious bodies who honour the Supreme Being "not to be hindered in their public teaching and witness to their faith" and stated that:

> Since the family is a society in its own right, it has the right freely to live its own domestic religious life under the guidance of parents. Parents, however, have the right to determine in accordance with their own religious beliefs the kind of religious education that their children are to receive.

Sin

Before we go on to outline the main lines of Catholic social teaching upon civil society, industrial relations, international relations and the use of force, it is essential to remember that the whole task of creating a social order which serves the real needs of mankind at every level is conditioned by sin. It is with a fallen race of men that we have to deal and a world vitiated both by original sin, of which the evidence is only too clamant, and the consequences of numberless actual sins against the law

---

46. *Sapientiae Christianae*, 1890.

and love of God day by day. Because of this, utopian schemes of a perfect human society upon which so many words have been wasted, are, of necessity, quite useless.

It is logical to discuss the practical problems of human society, as Christian philosophers like St. Thomas Aquinas are accustomed to do, in terms of the natural law, itself the creation of the Divine Mind. But the Church can never ignore or belittle the need of supernatural grace and the central, not occasional or accidental, importance of the Incarnate God in the contemporary world. Love of God and love of one's neighbour for God's sake remain indispensable to any real betterment of the human condition. That is why the idea that the existing evils of society can be remedied by political violence is a shallow illusion.

The Rule of Law

Yet while the power of human sin cannot be excluded from the present order of the world, it is evident that it must be contained and controlled if society is to persist and that a standard of right must be upheld. *Lex venit ob peccatum,* law came because of sin, is a conclusion as true as ever, though unpopular with the moderns. For, if there had been no original sin of our first parents, there would be no envy, no malice, no greed and no violence in the world. And so, to the positive elements of the natural law concerning everyone's right to life and to develop according to his genius, the integrity of the family, social charity and the sanctity of promises, were added through the protective experience of human societies a variety of prohibitive laws, the essentials of which, divested of their crudeness and cruelty, were revealed by Almighty God to Moses in the Decalogue. Those Commandments were, as we have seen, repeated and interpreted by Jesus Christ and completed by his law of love. Thus all society is, in the Christian conception, *subject to the rule of law;* the natural moral law as a universal obligation, the positive laws of civil authorities in so far as they do not violate the postulates of natural morality.

Authority

St. Thomas taught that "authority is the form of society," as the soul informs the human person, without which the body would be (as it is when the soul leaves it) inert matter. The Second Vatican Council, without saying so in so many words, relates the need for civil authority, like the law itself, to sin when it says:

> If the political community is not to be torn in pieces as each man follows his own viewpoint, authority is needed. This authority must dispose the energies of the whole citizens to the common good, not mechanically or despotically, but primarily as a moral force which depends on freedom . . .

It goes on to show that the political community and civil authority "belong to an order of things divinely foreordained" which is no doubt a modern way of saying, as did the apostles, that all authority comes from God, a truth which applies not only to the supreme rulers of the State, but also to fathers of familes and the heads of any human institutions like religious communities or schools, according to their function and degree. In the State "the choice of those who are to exercise authority is left to the free will of the citizens":

> It also follows that political authority, whether in the community as such or in institutions representing the State, must always be exercised within the limits of morality and on behalf of the dynamically conceived common good, according to a juridical order enjoying legal status. When such is the case citizens are in conscience bound to obey.[47]

Upon the very important qualification of authority operating within a clearly defined legal order, Pius XII had this to say at a time when the excesses of the totalitarian state were notorious:

> The relation of men towards men, of individuals towards society and authority and civic duties, and the relation of society and

---

47. *Gaudium et Spes.*

authority towards individuals—all these must be based upon a clear juridical foundation and where necessary, protected by the authority of the courts. This supposes a) a tribunal and a judge taking their directions from laws clearly defined; b) clear legal principles which cannot be upset by unwarranted appeals to a supposed popular sentiment or by merely utilitarian considerations; c) the recognition of the principle that the State also, and the officials and organisations dependent upon the State, are under the obligation of revising and withdrawing such measures as are incompatible with the liberty, the property, the honour, the advancement and the welfare of individuals.[48]

This somewhat detailed application of the rule of law required in the Christian social order is a good example of the care taken by modern popes to work out the necessary protection of the integrity of the human person against abuses of political power. This is the very opposite of the subordination of law to the racial policies of the Nazis, or the destruction of fair legal process which is inherent in "revolutionary justice," such as the Russian and Chinese show trials, or the revolutionary lynch law of Mr. Sekou Touré.

---

48. Pius XII, Christmas Message, 1942.

Chapter 11
ETHICS OF COMMUNITY RELATIONS

Industrial Relations

It is the encyclical *Rerum Novarum* of Leo XIII (1891) on industrial relations and especially the human rights of the workers that began the systematic social teaching of the Church in the modern world. All Leo's successors in the Holy See have not only referred to this encyclical as a landmark but repeated and expounded its principles, taking account of developments in society. Pius XI commemorating its fortieth anniversary in *Quadragesimo Anno;* Pius XII its fiftieth anniversary; John XXIII with the most extensive synthesis and extension of Leo's teaching in *Mater et Magistra;* Paul VI its eightieth anniversary—all (except, of course, the latter) formed the groundwork of the Second Vatican Council's treatment of the subject. There has thus grown up an impressive corpus of teaching which is the positive Christian alternative both to revolution and to tyranny, based upon those basic concepts of the intrinsic worth of the human person and the family which we have noticed above; based also on the need of conciliating these concepts with the common good, taking account of the complexities and varieties of economic life. Here we can only recall the principal guidelines.

First, there is the dignity of labour. It must never be treated as a mere commodity and its value measured, like that of merchandise, by the operation of the market. It is an activity reflecting man's skill and individuality, and must be regulated by standards of justice and equity. Secondly, private ownership even of capital goods is man's natural right: "There is a social function inherent in private ownership and therefore whoever in any way enjoys the right must do so for the benefit of others as well as himself."[49] In the concrete this refers to the person or company owning an industrial enterprise on the one hand, and on the other to the workers in it whose wages should help them to gain property of their own. Wages, fixed by a contract freely negotiated which must be honoured on both sides, must be the first claim on a firm's profit. "The wage paid to the worker must be sufficient to enable him to live a decent human life and to provide suitably for his family." The duty of the state, Pope Leo taught, is to "take care both that contracts of employment accord with the standards of justice and equity and that working conditions do not offend against the dignity of the human person, whether in his body or in his soul."[50] An impressive body of legislation has developed in all civilised countries since the 1890's to give effect to these principles.

Trade Unions

Then comes the right of association. *Rerum Novarum* states that "working men have a natural right to organise themselves into associations whether of themselves only or jointly with their employers" (the latter alternative was developed in some detail by Pius XI in *Quadragesimo Anno* but had few lasting results except in Portugal), and goes on to say that "all workers so organised in unions have the right to look after their interests in freedom and as they themselves desire, without having others obtrude into their affairs." What a contrast this is not only to the fitful and on the whole unsuccessful attempts of governments in capitalist states to obtrude, but to the total control of trade unions in the socialist bloc by the Communist Party.

---

49. *Mater et Magistra*, 19.
50. *Ibid.* 21.

Finally, Leo XIII expresses total opposition to class war as a means of advancing the workers' welfare:

> Workers and employers should respect the principles of human solidarity in organising their mutual relations and live together as befits Christians and brothers; for both that unlimited competition which is preached by Liberals, as they are called, and the class struggle which is a dogma of the Marxist, are plainly no less contrary to Christian teaching than they are to human nature itself.

"These," writes Pope John, summing up Leo's teaching, "are the foundations on which a sound economic and social order is to be built."[51]

Among various proposals put forward by the popes for giving effect to this principle of solidarity instead of antagonism between employers and employed are those of corporations or organized vocational groups which, as we have seen, have not been realised except, very gradually, in Portugal, and the more realistic idea of the workers participating in shareholding and even management in the firms for which they work. John XXIII was eloquent on that subject. This principle has found no favour in American industry but was applied with some vigour by President de Gaulle and now operates in a number of important French and German firms. It has been endorsed by the European Economic Community.

If we follow the many practical and detailed suggestions of Popes John XXIII and Paul VI concerning the application and amplification of these principles to the many economic problems of the changing world in which the advance of science and technology contributes to greater material wealth and social security in the advanced nations while it underlines the relative poverty of the underdeveloped, we are struck by the fact that the emphasis is overwhelmingly on the side of the "underdog." This is right and inevitable for a religion whose chief mission is to the multitude and the poor. But the under-

---

51. *Ibid.* 22–24.

dogs have a way of becoming top dogs in due course, and this sometimes distorts the papal championship of the erstwhile underprivileged. Condemnations of the worst aspects of capitalism are not lacking. Thus John XXIII quoting *Quadragesimo Anno* writes:

> Immense riches carrying with them corresponding power were being concentrated in the hands of a few who for the most part were not the owners, but only the trustees and directors of invested funds, which they administer at their own good pleasure . . . economic domination has taken the place of the open market.

But we look in vain for criticisms of trade union leaders. The fact that trade unions controlled by socialist militants may themselves become so powerful as to be the bullies of the community, as they are in danger of being in Britain, Italy and other Western countries, was unforeseen when the earlier papal documents were written.

The Ethics of the Strike

According to Catholic social teaching workers have the right to strike, either individually or collectively, as a means of defending their rights, for instance, against any breach of contract by the employer, unfair treatment, the withholding of just wages or pensions, unsafe or insanitary working conditions. In regard to the determination of a just wage for the worker with family obligations, it is evident that rising costs of living must be taken into account, having regard to the viability of the enterprise and the common good. But, as in the case of war or rebellion, a strike should always be the last resort, after every effort has been made at negotiation or mediation and for a cause sufficiently grave to justify the harm done to the workers themselves, their families, and innocent third parties. The sympathetic strike is more difficult to justify except in the case of collusion between one employer and another who has acted unjustly to nullify the strike against him. Father Paul Crane, S.J., in a recent study

134

of this subject,[52] holds that the same principles which determine the conditions of military intervention apply to the sympathetic strike:

> It is one thing for a nation to come to the aid of another against an unjust aggressor. This it may do under certain circumstances. But it is quite another for it to wage war against innocent third parties in the hope that thereby it will in some way indirectly help the victim of aggression. This it may never do for the end does not justify the means.

Still less can the purely political strike be justified in which industrial action is taken not because of a grievance against employers but to challenge the authority of lawful government. On one notorious occasion of this kind, the General Strike of 1926 in Britain, Cardinal Bourne, the Archbishop of Westminster, mounted his pulpit and said:

> There is no moral justification for a general strike of this character. It is a direct challenge to lawfully constituted authority and inflicts, without adequate reason, immense discomfort and injury on millions of our fellow countrymen. It is therefore a sin against the obedience which we owe to Almighty God who is the Source of that authority and against the charity and brotherly love which are due to our brethren.

It was widely held that this intervention helped to bring the strike to an end, though it implied no judgment on the case of the miners, in support of whom the general stoppage had been organized.

Our conclusion must therefore be that the Holy See has rendered a great service to humanity in laying down the right principles of economic life and tracing the ideals of human behaviour; but that the persistence of the revolutionary in penetrating even the most desirable human organisations has been greatly underestimated, and that it depends upon active Christians in each country to defend the right principles.

---

52. *Christian Order*, June 1973.

But though the question of industrial relations is the most familiar because the original subject of papal social teaching, it must be remembered that there are many other aspects of social life with which it is concerned—the particular problems of farmers for instance and the needs of depressed areas more especially of the developing nations, the particular object of Paul VI's devotion. In all these areas, it is the reality and compelling obligation of the fraternity of the human race which is the guiding principle.

International Relations

Since a special study is devoted below to the rights and wrongs of force in public life, we shall trace here only the main principles of international society taught by the Church.

The first principle indeed is that the world *is* a society. Not only does the common nature of all mankind establish a real human fraternity overriding political divisions and ethnic differences, but there is a natural society of nations, that is, of the political societies or states which are in existence at any given time, and also of less formal national entities not always identified with political frontiers. No one state or nation is so self-sufficient that it does not need for its security and development communication, cooperation and commercial intercourse with others. And because states and nations are simply collectivities of human beings, each subject in conscience to the moral law of God and especially of the requirements of justice and charity, it is these same moral imperatives that must govern their relations with one another on the world stage. They are inevitably members of a greater whole, namely the natural community of the world. They have their mutual rights and duties and an overriding obligation to contribute to the common good of the whole community. The keeping of faith between them, *pacta sunt servanda*, is the minimum basis of their moral bond of union. As Leo XIII put it, "That which is not permitted in private life is no less prohibited in public life."[53] Upon this, in

---

53. Encyclical *Longinqua Oceani*, 1895.

the mind of the Church, depends the whole prospect of a peaceful order.

> If order amongst states is to be securely established it must rest on the bedrock of these unalterable standards of honesty which the Creator has made to appear in nature itself and established irrevocably in the minds of men.[54]

It is on this fundamental conception of a natural society of nations that are based on the one hand the whole edifice of positive international law, treaties and conventions according to the practical needs of the times; on the other, the great contribution which the Christian spirit of charity has to offer to complement the requirements of strict justice, especially in the realms of conciliation, compassion, forgiveness of injuries, aid to the suffering, and mutual tolerance.

It is important also to remember that all we have noticed above concerning the State's regard for the human rights of the person and the family, private property, education, etc. (since, in the Catholic view, it applies to all states) is of common concern to all and thus becomes an end of the natural society of nations itself. The Universal Declaration of Human Rights, praised by Pope John XXIII, is an expression of that objective.

World Government

If such is the society established by nature among all peoples, there is a logical case for building upon it a positive society, giving legal form to its members' obligations, endowing it with authority and common organs. It was a long time after the breakdown of Christendom as a framework for the known world of European civilisation before attempts were made to establish this positive world society, first in the League of Nations, next in the United Nations. As for the popes, the main line of thought followed for over a century was the argument for the *inevitable* evolution of an organised society of the human race because of its ever growing economic interdepend-

---

54. *Ibid.*

ence (ethnarchy, it was called by Father Taparelli d'Azeglio, S.J., who developed the idea in his remarkable *Theoretic Essay of the Natural Law* in 1846). The latest and most complete conclusion of the argument is to be found in John XXIII's encyclical *Pacem in Terris*, in which he makes the case not only for improved *international* machinery but for a single world authority. International assemblies, treaties and conventions, he held, are no longer adequate means to provide security and peace or to satisfy the multifarious needs of the common good of mankind:

> Today the common good of all nations involves problems that affect people all the world over. These problems can be solved only by a public authority which has the power, the form and the competent agencies for dealing with them and whose sphere of influence is the entire globe. We cannot, therefore, escape the conclusion that the moral order itself demands the establishment of some sort of world government.

The experience of the United Nations does not suggest that this ideal is likely to be attained in the foreseeable future; and for a reason which, it would seem, frustrates the logical development of Taparelli's theory. That theory of the inevitable development of world society assumed the acceptance by its component states of the universal natural law. It was not an unreasonable assumption in the days of the Concert of Europe, during which the Jesuit wrote. A semblance of the idea survived to give a certain reality to the Covenant of the League of Nations in 1919, basically European as it was in composition. For however erroneous or egotistical might be from time to time the policies of the European powers, they inherited as a powerful legacy from their Christian history the sense of belonging to a common unity. It is the presence within the would-be world society today of many states who do not share that legacy, but most of all of powerful superstates whose basic philosophy denies the existence of an objective moral law superior to the interests of class and of the world revolution, which destroys the prospects of achieving a world government with the necessary moral authority.

Clearly there are advantages in established governments,

weak or powerful, meeting for discussion, taking common action when (as occasionally happens in the Security Council) their interests coincide, cooperating in various agencies in the various ways that their technical interdependence dictates. It is indeed arguable that the reality of the natural law and its obligations may gradually come into their own through the experience of this functional cooperation.

The contribution of Christian teaching and action to international relations is, however, by no means confined to this organizational speculation. It is through belief in the real, natural unity of the human family that the popes not only preach and plead for peace at every level but base their urgent insistence upon the duty of the more advanced and favoured members of the family to aid the development of its poorer and backward members. The notion that violent revolution or war is the means to achieve that purpose is wholly repugnant to the basic Christian conception of the Divine Fatherhood and the inescapable brotherhood of men.

Nationalism

Nationalism is the dominant political force in the world today. It is the basic determinant of all foreign policies, a potential dissolvent of unity in states containing more than one nationality and, through the consecration of "national self-determination" in the United Nations, the cause of the atomisation of the world community into the exclusive pattern of sovereign nation states. It has been powerful enough to induce the Universal Church to nationalise its liturgy and its hierarchical structure.

Nationalism arouses passions which, as we have seen, make it the favourite implement of Communism (outside the Soviet Union, where non-Russian nationalism is firmly suppressed) wherever it can serve to disintegrate political society or to advance revolutionary power (e.g. the ETA in Spain and the IRA in Ireland). "National liberation movements" was a formula invented as long ago as 1935 by the Comintern. It was first used in a big way to exploit the resistance forces in occupied Europe during World War II, later to secure control of subversive campaigns in the decolonisation era. Yet though nationalism, when it exalts the claims and ambitions of one nation at the expence of the rights of other nations and of the common good, is an anti-social evil, it is the outcome of a phenomenon which in itself is an essential part of the natural order and worthy of the highest respect.

Nation and State are not identical, though the vulgar practice of calling all states "nations," which came in with the League of Nations after the first World War and was inherited by the United Nations, confuses the two. Both communities are essential to minister to the needs of men as social beings. The State is a political organ whose function is order. It is necessary to protect and promote the welfare of all who live within its frontiers and to provide a just rule of law for them. The nation is a cultural community. As the word implies, it is a society in which one belongs by birth. It displays those characteristics of the family—religion, language, custom and tradition—which we have noticed above and which it shares with other families having a common historic association. These characteristics distinguish the group from other nations large or small, each of which has a different cultural heritage of its own. It is imbedded in the Christian philosophy to cherish and honour that heritage which is the natural framework of every man's life. It should always be respected and protected by law, whether the national group be a minority or a majority in the State. What constitutes a nation, whether of one ethnic stock (as in certain old European and Asian nations) or of mixed origins (as in the United States of America and other countries of new settlement) is *le vouloir vivre collectif,* the will to live together as a unit.

When nation and State coalesce, there is no conflict in the service which each renders to human personality and no conflict of loyalties. But it is necessary to remember that each is only of relative value. Men and women have many associations and interests, religious, intellectual, artistic and scientific, which overstep national frontiers. There is nothing absolute in "national self-determination," the demagogic slogan which President Woodrow Wilson bequeathed to the world. Stimulated by the escalation of nationalism in the French Revolution, the leaders of a number of old European nationalities secured statehood for their people chiefly through the break-up of the Ottoman and Habsburg Empires. This aspiration to political sovereignty, exported to other continents, became the objective of every national politician in territories where, from the middle of the 20th century, the colonial powers abdicated their authority. Many of the successor states, consisting of sections of tribes or of several warring tribes within arbitrarily traced colonial frontiers (e.g. Sudan, Nigeria, Zaire, Burundi) cannot by any stretch of imagination be described as nations. They may indeed *become* nations in the course of time and, for the sake of human lives, it is devoutly to be hoped that they will. The Church, Leo XIII wrote, "is not opposed to a nation becoming independent of any foreign or despotic power if it can be done without violation of justice." [55] His successors, including Benedict XV who insisted upon the restoration of Polish and Belgian independence in his letter to the belligerents in August 1917, have on the whole favoured national claims to political independence; and John XXIII and Paul VI have written of the independence of nearly all the ex-colonial peoples with evident approval.

But it must be remembered that many nations in the proper sense of the word are not now, and are not likely to become, sovereign states, nor would it be desired by the majority of their members. Thus there are three nations in the United Kingdom, three in Switzerland, four at least in Yugoslavia, two in New Zealand, two among others in Canada. Nor is there any reason why, if people are living together contentedly in a multiracial state, they should be compelled, because of the prevailing slogans of anti-colonial hatred, to be corralled into racial states. The Christian sense of social ethics understands the value of nationalism, but keeps it in its place. Humanity is much more important.

---

55. *Libertas Praestantissimum,* 1888.

Chapter 12

FORCE: RIGHT AND WRONG

It remains for us to define whether and in what circumstances right reason and Christian imperatives justify the use of armed force in civil society. The guiding principles of Catholic tradition on this subject have been implied in earlier parts of this book but it will be well to end our study by making clear the criterion by which the arguments for the cult of the Revolution must be judged.

The first priority is sacredness of human life. The universal instinct of self-preservation, the Divine Commandment "Thou shalt not kill," and Our Lord's instruction not to render evil for evil but to love our enemies, all combine to create a fundamental aversion to the taking of human life. Further, it is not the crude act of killing that is alone condemned; there is involved also, as Christ made clear in his Sermon on the Mount, the hatred and contempt of our brethren which leads to killing. To St. Augustine the worst of war is not "the death of those who must die sooner or later" (he is referring to soldiers who do their duty); "It is the desire of harming, the cruelty of avenging, the unruly and implacable animosity, the rage of rebellion, the lust of domination and the like—these are the things which are to be condemned in war."[56] Indeed, as all experience shows, the slaughter of man by man, whether it be the individual sin of murder or the organised killing involved in civil or international war, invariably implies a host of other evils. Thus it is the first duty of reasonable men and most of all of Chris-

---

56. *Contra Faustum*

tians not only to maintain peace, even an imperfect peace, but to prevent situations which may lead to violent subversion and its repression or to international war.

Yet the manifest existence in this sinful world of violent and anti-social elements within civil society—not excluding unjust oppression—and of conflicts between national interests and incompatible ideologies, makes it evidently necessary to use, on occasion, and to be prepared to use, force for the suppression of disorders and the defence of justice. This is indeed a duty which civil authority—and loyal citizens—cannot escape.

But because of our first and essential point, Christianity and right reason alike demand that occasions, even justifiable occasions, for initiating armed insurrection or intervention or, for that matter, violence by the police should not be sought out, still less exaggerated, over against the primary obligation to maintain or make peace. The use of armed force should only be resorted to in the case of real necessity. Yet this spirit is exactly the opposite of that of the Communist revolutionary and his allies among socialists and certain religious leaders, who use every device of *selectio veri suggestio falsi* and special pleading to justify so-called wars of liberation in Asia or Africa or to support guerrillas in Latin America rather than consider the practical possibilities of agreement. The spirit of the militant trade union leader, determined to prolong a damaging strike with no interest in a reasonable settlement, is equally un-Christian.

Because of this primary regard for the sacredness of human life, it has always been the practise of responsible Christian authorities from the generation in which the Church had to face, with the conversion of the Roman Empire, the responsibilities of civil society, to determine as strictly as possible the conditions under which force may be used in the service of justice. In so doing they had often to argue from the first principles of natural philosophy as well as from the Hebrew and Christian Scriptures; and their conclusions hold good regardless of the passage of time. Thus the principle that "It is always lawful to repel force by force" was accepted: that is, the natural right of self-defence. To this was added by St. Ambrose in the 4th century the social complement, that it is wrong to

144

fail to defend one's fellow against injury if one has the power to do so:[57] that is, the principle of intervention.

There followed the substantial teaching on the ethics of war in the writing of St. Augustine of Hippo.

The Ethics of War

"The just man," Augustine wrote, "should have no concern about this matter other than this. Is the war which is to be undertaken a just war?" He implies in many places that defence against invaders is a just war. For the rest he accepts the definition that "just wars are those which avenge injuries . . . or are fought to recover what has been unjustly taken by a nation or city." [58] Again: "It is the wrongdoing of the opposing party which obliges the just man to wage just wars." Here is the beginning of those conditions for a just war to which so much attention was given by the theologians of later centuries and which have become increasingly restrictive; but the main point of St. Augustine's teaching is that only as a means of restoring peace can war be right. His most famous sentences on this are in his letter to Count Boniface, the Roman Governor of Northern Africa (c. A.D. 418):

> Peace should be the object of your desire; war should be waged only as a necessity, and waged only that God may by it deliver men from that necessity and preserve them in peace . . . Therefore, even in waging war, be a peacemaker (esto bellando pacificus), that by defeating those against whom you are fighting, you may lead them back to the advantages of peace.

Is this really old-fashioned? Or is it not what the civilised military commander or police officer today, called upon to restore order, knows to be his rational purpose?

The conditions for a legitimate recourse to war, evolved from this early Christian thinking, apply to the initiation of hostilities rather than to defence against actual aggression,

---

57. *Qui non repellit injuriam a socio, si potest, tam est in vitio quam ille qui fecit. De Officiis.*

58. *Commentary on the Book of Numbers.*

which requires no justification. They were summarised as follows in the revised Code of International Ethics drawn up by the International Union of Social Studies (the Malines Union):[59] For a war to be lawful; it must a) have been declared by a legitimate authority; b) have a just and grave cause, proportioned to the evils which it brings about; c) be undertaken only after all means of peaceful solution of the conflict have been exhausted without success; d) have serious chances of success; e) be carried out with a right intention.

It is rare nowadays, with the opportunities for conciliation, mediation or arbitration which the development of the international community provide (notably the provisions of the United Nations Charter if they were properly used), for a justifiable cause of international war to be other than a country's defence against actual aggression, or the intervention by another state or several states to help the victim of aggression. But there are still parts of the world where irredentism, i.e., the claim to recover territory believed to have been unjustly seized in the past,[60] is a very possible argument for war. These logical "conditions" therefore retain their validity. The last four of them are, as we shall see, basically the same as those required to make an armed insurrection legitimate.

The first is a necessity for positive international law, to determine the rights and limitations of belligerents and neutrals. It also embodies the important principle which every organised state has adopted internally, namely that individuals and lesser groups within the state, be they feudal lords, national minorities or political factions, must not take the law into their hands by using violence in their sectional interests. Since to make war is the gravest of political decisions, Christian tradition has always insisted that it must be only the supreme authority in the State (after due civic process and examination of the justice of the cause) which may take this responsibility, and international law necessarily holds the belligerent government re-

---

59. English edition (which I translated and edited), Newman Press, Westminster, Md., 1953.

60. The Arab case against Israel is a striking example.

146

sponsible for all the warlike operations of its armed forces and citizens, as well as for the observance of the international conventions designed to limit the horrors of war which it has signed.

The Second Vatican Council[61] described the savagery of war today as "far surpassing that of the past" including "guerrilla warfare extended by new methods of deceit and subversion. In many cases the use of terrorism is regarded as a new way of waging war." In view of this melancholy state of affairs the Council wished "to recall first of all the permanent binding force of universal natural law and its all-embracing principles." Therefore, "actions which deliberately conflict with these same principles as well as orders commanding such actions are criminal. Blind obedience cannot excuse those who yield to them." Genocide is vehemently condemned. "International agreements aimed at making military activity and its consequences less inhuman must be honoured and improved upon." Though the Council insists that "it is our clear duty to strain every muscle as we work for the time when all war can be completely outlawed by international consent" (a consummation as desirable as it is improbable), it realises that "war has not been rooted out of human affairs." It does not specify the conditions for applying to it the principles of the universal natural law, except for the case of natural self-defence:

> As long as the danger of war remains and there is no competent and sufficiently powerful authority at the international level, governments cannot be denied the right of legitimate defence once every means of peaceful settlement have been exhausted. Therefore, government authorities and others who share public responsibility have the duty to protect the welfare of the people entrusted to their care. . . .
>
> Those who are pledged to the service of their country as members of its armed forces should regard themselves as agents of security and freedom on behalf of their people. As long as they fulfil this role properly, they are making a genuine contribution to the establishment of peace.

---

61. *Gaudium et Spes.*

Thus the Augustinian doctrine prevails.

While wars of subversion are included in the general observations of this chapter of the Council's Constitution *Gaudium et Spes* dealing with war, the specific problems posed by organised campaigns of subversion and revolution are not faced.

The Ethics of Rebellion

The "conditions of just rebellion" have been conscientiously studied and defined by moral theologians no less than the conditions of international war. There is no question that a government which consistently violates the natural law from which it derives its right to govern forfeits its authority. The following statement of Leo XIII[62] is a good example of the way in which the Church combines the overriding duty of obedience to authority for the sake of the common good with the duty of disobedience if the worst comes to the worst:

> Should it happen at any time that in the public exercise of authority rulers act rashly and arbitrarily, the teaching of the Catholic Church does not allow subjects to rise against them without further warranty, lest peace and order become more and more disturbed and society run the risk of greater detriment. And when things have come to such a pass as to hold out no further hope, she teaches that a remedy is to be sought in the virtue of Christian patience and in urgent prayer to God. But should it please legislators to enjoin or sanction anything repugnant to the divine and natural law, the dignity and duty of the name of Christian and the Apostolic injunction proclaim that we *ought to obey God rather than men* (Acts V, 29).

(One might well ask whether the wholesale legalisation of abortion does not create such a crisis of loyalties.) This may be described as the minimal position concerning the right of collective disobedience to authority.

Pius XI made a clear distinction between a just and an unjust insurrection in his encyclical addressed to the Mexican hierarchy on 28 March 1937, at a time when religious and personal

---

62. *Quod Apostolica Muneris*, 28 December 1888.

liberties were subject to severe oppression by an anti-Christian government:

> You have more than once reminded your sons that the Church stands for peace and order, even at the cost of heavy sacrifices, and condemns every unjust insurrection or resort to violence against the established government. On the other hand you have also affirmed that, should that government itself revolt against justice and truth to the extent of destroying the very foundations of authority, one cannot see that it would be possible to blame the citizens for uniting to defend the nation and themselves, by lawful and appropriate means, against those who misuse public power to bring ruin to the country.

The ruling of the Second Vatican Council follows a similar line:

> When public authority oversteps its competence and oppresses the people, these people should nevertheless obey to the extent that the objective common good demands. Still, it is lawful for them to defend their own rights and those of their fellow citizens against any abuse of this authority, provided that in so doing they observe the limits imposed by natural law and the Gospel.

What are those limits? René Coste in his *Morale Internationale*[63] summarises the prevailing theological doctrine on the right of insurrection against a tyrannical government as follows:

> It can only be made lawful by the convergence of several conditions:
> —extremely grave abuses of political power;
> —the failure of all peaceful means to bring them to an end;
> —the lesser gravity of the calamities which will result from the insurrection compared with that of the injustices caused by the tyrannical government (the rule of the lesser evil);
> —reasonable prospects of success.

This last condition is of great moral importance when considering the case for recourse to either war or rebellion. For

---

63. Desclée, 1964.

if there be no well-founded probability of success, the unleashing of violence will simply mean condemning many people uselessly to death. This would be the case, for example, if the Baltic peoples engulfed in the Soviet Union were egged on to revolt with external assistance. It would be equally the case, in all probability, in the event of an attempt at violent subversion in the South African Republic. There are many situations where, for the sake of human lives, violence is worse than useless as a remedy for social evils. The great difficulty, of course, is how to calculate the prospects of success or failure and also to decide fairly whether a government is really tyrannical. St. Thomas, without defining tyranny, taught that a tyrannical government was unjust because it was no longer ordained to the public good and that the overthrow of such a government was not seditious "unless this overthrow could only be accomplished with such disorder that it would cause the country more damage than the tyranny itself." [64]

It is obvious, however, that in the interests of the men, women and children concerned, and not from any preconceived devotion to the *status quo,* the onus of proving the necessity of a violent disturbance rests on the advocates of revolution. A thoughtful report, *Civil Strife,* prepared by the Board of Social Responsibility of the General Synod of the Church of England in 1971 points out that:

> All government rests to some extent upon coercion as well as consent. It is only if the coercion is used to perpetrate injustice or is out of all proportion to the needs of government that violent revolution can be justified.

The report therefore gives the following definition of the requirements for a legitimate insurrection:

> The regime concerned must be palpably unjust and tyrannical; the oppression it employs must be out of all proportion to the needs of government, including external threats of security; every effort must have been made to seek a solution by negotiation

---

64. *Summa Theologica,* IIa IIae, qu. 42, arts. 2 & 3.

and conciliation; the good to be attained must be greater than the evils, material and spiritual, which will ensue; the rules of the Just War must, so far as possible, be observed; and there must be a reasonable chance of success.

This seems to me an admirable conclusion which it would be difficult to fault on grounds of right reason or humanity. The reference to the rules of Just War mean in the context, I believe, the rules for the conduct of hostilities by the belligerents of which the most important of all is that "it is never lawful deliberately to kill innocent people." This means, for instance, that the assassination of village headmen or other leaders by revolutionaries as a tactic of "selective terrorism" is unpardonable murder. It also means that the indiscriminate bombardment of populated areas in war with no regard for the lives of non-combatants is no less a crime, which is why weapons of mass destruction were unequivocally condemned by the Second Vatican Council. Then there are a number of treaties designed to mitigate the cruelties of war, beginning with those of the Hague Conferences of 1899 and 1907, which lay down, among other things, that "the rights of belligerents to adopt means of injuring the enemy are not unlimited"; that it is forbidden "to kill or wound an enemy who, having laid down his arms or having no longer means of defence, has surrendered at discretion"; "to declare that no quarter will be given"; or to force prisoners to take part in military operations against their own country. Other provisions protect the civil population under enemy occupation.

Stemming from the original Red Cross Convention on succour to the wounded of both sides, there is a whole body of international "Red Cross law" and projected law elaborated at recurrent conferences and concerned with the protection of prisoners of war, the wounded and other victims of war, the whole object of which is to protect the human person as far as possible. Concerned originally with its mission of mercy in interstate wars, the International Red Cross in four conventions signed at Geneva in August 1949 secured the inclusion of obligations arising from armed conflicts not of an international character (i.e., civil wars, resistance movements, etc.) on the territory of a contracting party. They provide, for instance, for the humane treatment of persons not directly involved in hostilities, the sick and the wounded. They forbid the infliction of personal injuries, torture, cruel punishments and death; the taking of hostages; and condemnations or executions without proper judicial trial, etc. In short, though some of these international conventions are in operation, others await sufficient ratifications. Still, there are well established rules which should be observed by governments, whether engaged in defending their country or resisting rebellion, and by insurgents engaged in a revolution they believe to be just.

Finally there is a rule for a just war which is of universal application. It is the rule of minimum force. Whether it be a question of the police coping with a rioting crowd or regular forces waging a justifiable war of defence or suppressing a rising, or an insurgent force believing that it has right on its side, it is an essential requirement of morality that only so much force should be used and such weapons employed as are necessary for the success of the action. This again is intended to limit as far as is reasonable the impact of force upon human beings.

How then does the notion of perpetual and ubiquitous revolution as a cure for the defects of human society fit into this reasonable philosophy of the use of force in the service of peace which centuries of Christian civilisation have evolved? There is no place for it. However the question be posed, there cannot be any case for the attempt to overthow the existing political and economic structure—meaning, of course, that of states outside the Communist orbit—without regard to the real differences and distinctive circumstances of time and place; and all sweeping generalities break down under honest examination. As we saw at the start of this study, while there may be an occasion when a violent upheaval is legitimate in the cause of justice, it is bound to be *exceptional* because of the vital need of ordinary people and their families for peace and stability; and it is only with regard to the particular conditions of a particular country at a particular turn of its affairs, that the merits or feasibility of such a revolution can be judged.

Those Catholics, therefore, who are committing themselves

to the myth of World Revolution and its slogans are bound before long to come adrift from the safe moorings of the Christian tradition of the moral law and objective truth, and to find themselves at sea with helmsmen who have nothing in common with the seamanship of Peter's successor. It is only as the crew and the puppets of the directing minds of Marxism-Leninism, with their set purpose, their dogmatic materialism, and their formula for power, that their Catholic followers are likely to find any place in the history of the 20th century.

INDEX

Titles of books and papal encyclicals are printed in italics.

155